Clodagh's Suppers

Clodagh's Suppers

SUPPERS TO CELEBRATE THE SEASONS

Clodagh McKenna

Photography by Dora Kazmierak

Kyle Books

This book is dedicated to my true love,
Harry Herbert.

An Hachette UK Company
www.hachette.co.uk

This edition published in 2019, first published in Great Britain
in 2019 by Kyle Books, an imprint of Kyle Cathie Ltd
Carmelite House
50 Victoria Embankment
London EC4Y 0DZ
www.kylebooks.co.uk

ISBN: 978 1 90948 799 4

Distributed in the US by Hachette Book Group, 1290 Avenue of
the Americas, 4th and 5th Floors, New York, NY 10104

Distributed in Canada by Canadian Manda Group,
664 Annette St., Toronto, Ontario, Canada M6S 2C8

Publisher: Joanna Copestick
Editor: Vicky Orchard
Design: Lucy Gowans
Creative director: Clodagh McKenna
Photography: Dora Kazmierak

Food styling: Lizzie Harris
Props styling: Wei Tang
Production: Nic Jones, Gemma John and Katherine Hockley

Printed and bound in China

10 9 8 7 6 5 4 3 2 1

Contents

Introduction

I am never happier than seeing my loved ones sitting around the table with smiles on their faces as they enjoy delicious home-cooked food in a beautiful setting. The importance of supper at home has been instilled in me since I was a child. I have so many amazing memories of suppers shared with my family when we were children—the table laid with proper linen, fresh flowers, and bowls of home-cooked food. The suppers nearly always ended with someone singing a song or one of us giving some sort of performance. This has now become a tradition at my suppers in my own home, sometimes even beginning before the main course hits the table! For me, this is what life is all about—enjoying memorable moments together. I truly hope that by sharing all my recipes, tips, tablescape ideas, menus, and cocktails that you will start hosting your own suppers at home.

I call it a supper rather than a dinner, and you may wonder what the difference is. For me, a supper is relaxed and informal—a delicious loaf of my Rosemary Clodagh Bread (page 203) on a wooden cutting board in the center of the table with hands diving in to tear chunks off to dip in a seasonal soup such as my Smoked Haddock & Corn Chowder (page 108). A supper is all about sharing food made by you around a table where your friends and family feel completely at home and relaxed.

I have created menus with an appetizer, main course, and dessert to give you an idea of which flavors work well together in a meal that is also balanced. I have planned them so that the courses aren't too laborious, and some you can even cook a day ahead to make it stress-free. You can also swap out the recipes to create the menu that you love best, but I would suggest trying to keep within the seasons, as the food will always taste and look better.

To kick off my suppers, I love to set up a cocktail table with one seasonal special, such as my Sparkling Rhubarb Cocktail (page 182) in the spring or the Blackberry & Rosemary Cocktail (page 186) in the fall. I also serve a delicious seasonal snack, such as the Spring Pea Guacamole with Radishes (page 191), on the table with the cocktails. Always a fun way to start the evening! In the summer, I will have this set up on a table with fresh flowers in the garden, and during the colder months, I'll create the cocktail area in a more cozy setting by the fire.

Every week I develop recipes in my kitchen for my weekly *Evening Standard* column and for television shows, such as Channel 4's *Sunday Brunch*, the NBC *Today* show, and *The Marilyn Denis Show* in Canada, as well as many others including my weekly Youtube series. So there are lots of recipes to test every week and my favorites always end up at my suppers at home, where my critics give their reviews for better or worse! I am so excited to share the 120 recipes that came out on top in the pages ahead. All the recipes have suggested curated supper menus, but of course there are many ideas for soups, salads, pâtés, one-pot suppers, cakes, and so on that are perfect for everyday cooking.

I have laid out the book to make it as simple as possible for you to find all that you need for creating the perfect supper at home! The first section is about the preparation, including a checklist of what you need to prepare before everyone arrives. This is followed by some beautiful seasonal tablescapes to give you lots of inspiration and ideas on how to easily turn your table into a visually spectacular setting. The second section focuses on the menu and recipes to help you create a well-balanced menu that suits each season and occasion. I have also included festive occasions such as Easter, Thanksgiving, and Christmas. Lastly, a chapter on cocktails and snacks will help you decide what to serve when your guests arrive as well as some delicious treats for after supper, like my Rosewater & Pistachio Florentines (page 194), which take just 15 minutes to make.

Creating a magical supper is so much fun and will fill your home with special memories. Plan it out so that it's not a stressful task but an enjoyable one where you can unleash your creative side. Sprigs of branches, herbs, or flowers along the table with ambient candles dotted through, dried lavender on everyone's napkins, or figs with place settings popped in a slit of the fruit, are all so easy to create. One delicious plate of homemade food is so much more special than three courses of store-bought meals. Keep it simple and cook the dishes that you love the most. Candles lit, playlist on, table laid, food cooked—all that's left is to make yourself one of my delicious cocktails and let it be a night to remember.

Happy Suppers!

Love Clo xx

The Menu

The menu is undoubtedly the most important part of my supper party, and I always carve out a bit of time to create a well-balanced menu with courses complementing each other. I love getting into bed early with a pen and paper a few nights before I host a supper and leisurely writing a menu that I will get excited about cooking.

IN SEASON

The first thing I do is write out a list of foods that are in season. This is so important to me because seasonal ingredients always taste so much better and I love being present with the passing of the seasons. It creates such a memorable occasion—indeed all the recipes in the pages ahead mark the seasons. Seeing the first of the rhubarb at the local farmer's market and making it into a syrup for a sparkling rhubarb cocktail—that first delicious sip has me right back to when I was a child and my mother would make butter pastry rhubarb tarts. That is exactly what suppers are all about for me—creating memories that will live on and on... Cooking with the seasons allows me to get excited about the coming months and the produce they will bring.

BALANCING THE MENU

When I am planning my supper, I start with the dish that I am most excited about cooking, and then I build around it. Here's what I always stick to: If I am cooking fish or something spicy for the main course, then I will tend to serve a light, refreshing dessert to cleanse the palate. To start the supper, a vegetable- or fish-based dish works very well, like my Gazpacho (page 71) or Crab, Blood Orange & Fennel Salad (page 154). When it comes to a meat-based main course, I serve soups or other light meat dishes. I am never in favor of spicy or creamy courses following one another—I wouldn't serve a cream-based dish after a chowder, as it would be too rich. The trick is for your guests' palates to be refreshed with different flavors after each course. The menu also goes with the season—I tend to eat more hearty foods in the winter (I think we all do!), so during the colder months you can get away with serving more filling courses throughout the supper. In the summer, we look for lighter, fresher-tasting foods since we don't crave the warming comfort dishes of the colder months.

The Prep

Once you have decided on your menu, the next thing to start thinking about is how to best prepare and get organized. Everyone knows how to write a grocery list, but it might also help to have a checklist of everything you need to do beforehand, from choosing the wine to creating a playlist and even to thinking about who's going to sit where. This is my helpful guide to everything you need to consider before your supper.

GROCERY LISTS

I am a bit of a list queen, it has been said... I like to be organized, and making lists is how I take the stress out of any task. When it comes to hosting a supper at home, the shopping can be the most mundane part of it. I separate my shopping list into two sections—dry ingredients and fresh ingredients. I go through my cupboards and check my stock of dry foods, candles, seltzer water, wine, etc., and then make my list. I generally order the dry ingredients online and have them delivered days before, which saves time and energy. The fresh ingredients I spend more time on; if it's fish that I am cooking, I take the time to go to a good fishmonger, as the better the quality, the better your cooking will taste! For meat, it is always worth the trip to a good butcher. If you are on a budget, then you'll have a better range of cheaper, less-used cuts from the butcher, which is also a great place to get bones for broths and stocks if you are making a soup or risotto. I shop for the fresh ingredients the day before.

TABLETOP WARE

Don't leave this until the last minute, or your guests could be eating off paper plates! Count how many guests you have for supper, then pull out all your dishes, cutlery, and glassware. Decide which dish you are going to use for each course and count how many you have to ensure there's enough for everyone. Do the same with your glassware, matching them to the wines and water you are serving, and finish by sorting the platters (if using) for serving the food.

HERE'S MY FOOLPROOF SUPPER CHECKLIST

• Count cutlery, dishes, and glassware

• Polish silverware and glassware

• Cocktail set up – ice, shaker, liquor, soda water, lemons, cocktail glasses, and tray

• Linen – napkins and tablecloth

• Two good playlists – one for before and during supper and one for after (if your suppers are like mine and you like a post-supper boogie!)

• Candlesticks and holders, cleaned and polished

• Candles for the table, around the house, and a nice smelling candle in the bathroom

• Vases for flowers, cleaned and ready for arranging

• Flowers for the table, around the house, and also a small arrangement beside the sink in the bathroom

• Water jugs filled with ice, mint, and lemon slices

• Butter sliced on small butter dishes with a little sprig of fresh rosemary

• Small bowls for sea salt

The Table

Along with creating the menu, styling the table is definitely one of my favorite parts of planning a supper. I love being able to transform my table into a space that reflects the seasons and the ingredients that I'm going to use. In this section, I share with you the best ways to create a beautifully set table that will make any supper even more special, and the great thing is that it can be done in advance, leaving you more time to enjoy cooking.

HANDWRITTEN MENUS

A handwritten menu perched in the middle of your table sets such a lovely personal tone. This can be done really simply by using nice postcards or 5 x 8-inch blank notecards. I always write them in pencil (easy to rub out mistakes) and draw little illustrations of vegetables or festive images along the side. The following day, I clip the menu on my menu string in my kitchen, as I love to stop and read back through them.

LINEN

Texture is important to create a beautiful table, and good linen will soften and warm hard textures such as wood or glass. It is worth investing in a good tablecloth and napkins that will last you through the years. I love natural linen, as the more you use and wash it, the better it becomes. I have four different sets of linen—one for each of the four seasons. Soft blush pink for summer, mustard for fall, teal green for winter, and soft sage green for spring. The linen for me is the canvas to the table, and I build upon that, introducing colors through flowers and dishes that will reflect the season and work with the linen. Linen napkins bring a softness to the table that you won't get from using paper. As well as linen, I have a drawer where I keep all different colors and textures of ribbon—these are to tie napkins with sprigs of seasonal flowers or herbs.

DISHES, CUTLERY, AND GLASSWARE

Most of my dishes, cutlery, and glassware come from secondhand stores and markets. This is the best place to pick up special pieces for your table without it costing a fortune. Don't worry about not getting matching sets—I love to mix and match, because it brings more personality to the table. Also keep an eye out for flower vases, jugs, and small bowls that can be used for sea salt, sauces, and butter.

I recently picked up a whole set of Irish china for $25 in a thrift store in Ireland, and these mixed store-bought plates look so pretty even though they don't match. It's well worth taking an afternoon to forage through a secondhand store to find treasures for your table.

FLOWERS

Like my food, I always use seasonal flowers. Seeing the seasons visually throughout my home makes me so happy, and on my table it creates a seasonal moment. The flowers are fresher, more pert, and usually cheaper when you buy in season. If you live in the country or you visit the country a lot, go and pick wild flowers if available. I do this most weekends. I like to use one to three types of flowers on a table, as any more in the mix makes it too busy. A lot of the time I just use one variety, even if it's just a simple bluebell in spring, because it makes a beautiful impact.

When I'm using just one variety of flower, I will use lots of them and place one to two stems in different-sized jars or vases around the table. I also place one on everyone's napkin as part of the place setting. Ivy running down the center of a rectangular table can look great, especially with little lights throughout and small jars of flowers. Big sprigs of tree branches look fantastic at the end of the table or on a sideboard—and you can do this at any time of the year. The idea is to bring as much seasonality to the supper table as possible.

The Table SPRING

For me, a spring table is all about adding freshness and vitality to the table. Beautiful shades of green with fresh white flowers and green stems are a staple during spring. Lots of stem vases with two or three wild garlic flowers or snowdrops look so pretty running down the center of the table, with a large vase in the center or to the side filled with large branches with buds about to open. Bluebells are such a pretty spring flower and look lovely in stem glasses or as a sprig on every napkin. A flood of daffodils can look really cheerful on a white linen tablecloth or as small bunches tied with twine on each napkin.

I also love decorating the table with seasonal vegetables. At this time of year, fresh radishes with their long, green leaves look fabulous dotted along the table, or again placed on each napkin. Green linen napkins, sage or olive, are my favorite shades during spring. They look beautiful on a wooden table or on a fresh white or cream linen tablecloth. Matching these with pewter plates or pottery looks stunning. A spring table with delicate, simple flowers and soft green seasonal colors really captures this special time of year and brightens up your home after a long winter.

The Table SUMMER

This summer table that I have created is dressed with a soft, blush pink, washed linen cloth. I then use blue and white Danish or Portuguese-style dishes with soft, blush pink, washed linen napkins folded on top and wrapped with pink velvet ribbon. I then insert the cutlery under the ribbon. Along the table I have single stems of peonies or tulips that look so delicate and pretty.

I also love picking wild flowers at this time of the year and creating a meadow-like feel for the table. Little bundles of cottage roses in between tealights in pretty glass jars or brass stem candles are so romantic.

When it comes to the end of the summer and heirloom tomatoes are available at farmers' markets, I also love to use those for decorating the table. The different colors and varieties of tomatoes look so beautiful. Soft, blue linen is also gorgeous in the summer, and if you are near the coast, do go and collect some pretty shells to place on pale blue napkins. Larger flat shells can also be used as butter, salt, and salsa dishes.

The Table FALL

Fall is my favorite table to create. Different shades of brown, mustard, and purple all look so stunning on the table. I love a mustard-colored linen tablecloth set off with lilac-colored linen napkins and small bunches of dried lavender sprigs tied together with twine. It reminds me of harvesttime in France. Big bunches of dried wheat in vases at each end of the table or the center, and other dried flowers in small vases scattered across the table also look beautiful. I tie small bunches of dried lavender on the backs of the chairs, which not only looks pretty, but also smells amazing.

Another great look is a blackberry sprig on each napkin with longer sprigs in vases along the table. There are also so many amazing varieties of small ornamental squashes that you can buy in your local vegetable store or market available in wonderful colors that look fantastic.

Another idea is to press brown leaves between books (so they don't curl up) and then place them on each table setting with acorns on top. They also make great name placeholders since you can write on them! Large fig leaves used as charger plates or in the center of the table under bowls or candles look fabulous, too.

The Table WINTER

Fresh figs, heather, pussy willows, red berry branches, pomegranates, and clementines are all in season during the winter months and will make any table look magical. In this setting, I am using my teal blue linen tablecloth and napkins, which not only give a lovely warmth but also go well with winter reds and the earthy colors of fresh figs and heather. I buy the heather in containers, keep them in the garden, then cut the sprigs when I need them to decorate my table. Simple bundles of heather tied together on a napkin look lovely. I also use fresh figs as table settings, and by making a slit halfway down (cutting from the top) you can pop name cards into them. Big beautiful sprigs of pussy willow look fabulous as a centerpiece to a winter table, with a few sprigs of red berry branches dotted throughout. Add a few fairy lights (battery powered) around them for instant festive ambience!

When I am planning my festive tables during the winter, I often use clementines to decorate the place settings. Try to find the ones with the green leaves on them so you can write your guests' names on the leaf. Arrange halved pomegranates along the table, as the jewels inside the fruit look pretty and festive. Finally, don't forget to add lots of candles to light up your Christmas table!

Ambience

LIGHTING

Besides the food, lighting is the most vital element of a supper. A brightly lit room is my idea of a total nightmare, as it makes me feel tired incredibly quickly and there is nothing relaxing about bright lights! It takes no time to quickly check the bulbs on your lamps, and there are many lovely soft light bulbs available. Next up, overhead lights never work for me, so just turn them off. Having had my own restaurants for many years, I firmly believe that most people don't like these either.

What I have learned is that you simply can't have too many candles! To be really picky, the flicker of a candle should be lower than your chin and not at eye-level or above as this creates the most flattering and soft light. This might sound a bit over the top, but it's always good to know when you are buying candlesticks. I adore brass candlesticks, which can be found on eBay or at secondhand stores. Also, have fun with colored candles—my favorites are natural wax, but I also love olive green and blush pink, which can really add to the look of the table. Don't forget about the area surrounding your table, such as mantelpieces, side tables, and drinks cabinets. Floods of tealights in brown paper bags or glass jars at the entrance or around the yard can look gorgeous, but remember to put out quite a few either dotted in a line or bundled together to make an impact.

COMFORT

The seating is so important for your guests to enjoy a comfortable evening. If your dining chairs are hard, then the easiest thing to do is put cushions on them. I like all my cushion covers to match and for the color to be neutral so that it will go well with all my different tablecloths. My cushions are white with navy pinstripes, and I have 20 of them for larger suppers. The next thing is warmth. When I am having a supper in the garden, I drape wraps, pashminas, or small blankets over the backs of chairs. It's lovely for your guests not to worry about getting chilly and it keeps the party going on longer! Plus it looks lovely.

MUSIC

If you follow me on social media, or have been to my house for supper, then you will know already how much I love music and a good boogie or sing-along after supper! I like to have three playlists ready—something jazzy or Motown (Nina Simone is a favorite or nothing beats the Buena Vista Social Club) for cocktails upon arrival, something more folksy such as Hozier for supper, and post-supper, the playlist should be either fun sing-alongs or for dancing—Tina Turner is always on my list. Be sure to take some time out to create your playlist a week before you host your supper, as it's fun and it adds a wonderful ambience.

Spring Suppers

Menus

SPRING SUPPER FOR TWO

SOFT-BOILED EGG WITH CRUMBLED
BLOOD SAUSAGE & ASPARAGUS

LOBSTER LINGUINE

MY ITALIAN BAKED RICOTTA CHEESECAKE

SPRING ROAST LAMB SUPPER

WATERCRESS SOUP WITH ROSEMARY
& TOASTED PINE NUTS

ROAST BUTTERFLIED LAMB
WITH SALSA VERDE

LEMON MERINGUE PIE

WILD GARLIC FOREST SUPPER

WILD GARLIC SOUP WITH TOASTED
ALMONDS & SHEEP CHEESE

WILD GARLIC TAGLIATELLE WITH
GOAT CHEESE, ZUCCHINI
& TOASTED ALMONDS

COCONUT & LEMON CLOUD CAKE

ST. PATRICK'S DAY SUPPER

SALT-BAKED POTATO WITH CRÈME
FRAÎCHE & TROUT CAVIAR

SODA-BREADED PORK CHOPS WITH IRISH
HONEY & WHISKEY DIP & COLCANNON

GUINNESS CARAMEL TIRAMISU

EASTER SUPPER

SPRING PEA, PEA SHOOT, PANCETTA &
GOAT CHEESE SALAD

HAZELNUT & HERB-CRUSTED
LAMB CUTLETS WITH PEA & WILD
GARLIC PURÉE

RHUBARB, ROSEWATER & PISTACHIO
GALETTES

FISH SUPPER

DUBLIN BAY PRAWN CEVICHE

SEA BREAM & CLAMS WITH PURPLE
SPROUTING BROCCOLI, ROMESCO
& CRUNCHY SEEDS

LEMON VERBENA POSSETS

SPRING GATHERING

ASPARAGUS MIMOSA

WATERCRESS BUTTERED CHICKEN WITH
FAVA BEANS & ROSEMARY POTATOES

RHUBARB & CRYSTALLIZED GINGER
UPSIDE-DOWN CAKE

Wild Garlic Soup with Toasted Almonds & Sheep Cheese

SERVES 6

This wild garlic soup is so deliciously pungent, just one spoonful transports me back to the forest floor of wild garlic where I picked it. I have added a topping of toasted almonds and sheep cheese for texture and a contrast of flavor. You could use hazelnuts, Brazil nuts, or pine nuts instead of the almonds, and during other seasons, you can replace the wild garlic with spinach, watercress, or wild nettle tops.

3 tablespoons butter

2 cups potatoes, peeled and coarsely chopped

$^2/_3$ cup onions, coarsely chopped

$4^1/_4$ cups hot chicken or vegetable stock

7 ounces wild garlic leaves, thoroughly washed and chopped

sea salt and freshly ground black pepper

$^1/_2$ cup heavy cream

FOR THE TOPPING

$^1/_2$ cup toasted almonds, chopped

$^1/_2$ cup sheep cheese, such as feta, crumbled

$^1/_3$ cup extra virgin olive oil

wild garlic flowers, thoroughly washed, to garnish

Place a heavy-bottomed saucepan over medium heat and add the butter. Once the butter has melted, add the potatoes and onions, stir well, and cover the pan with a lid. Reduce the heat to low and leave the vegetables to sweat for about 10 minutes, stirring occasionally.

Add the hot stock and wild garlic leaves and bring to a boil, then reduce the heat and simmer, uncovered, for about 10 minutes until the potatoes are tender.

Transfer the soup to a blender or food processor, or use an immersion blender, and process to a smooth consistency.

Return the soup to the saucepan (if necessary) and season with salt and pepper. Stir in the cream and place over medium heat for just 2 minutes to warm through.

Meanwhile, for the topping, mix the almonds, sheep cheese, and extra virgin olive oil together in a small bowl.

Pour the soup into warmed bowls, spoon the almond and sheep cheese mixture on top of each serving, and sprinkle with wild garlic flowers to garnish.

Asparagus Mimosa

These green spears look beautiful on the table. Plus, the combination of the roasted asparagus with the fluffy hard-boiled egg flecked on top, finished with the sweet and citrusy flavors of the lemon and basil in the dressing, is so delicious! You can serve this up on one or two big platters if you are feeding a large crowd, and the eggs and dressing can be prepared the day before, so it's an easy appetizer to pull together. I've also made this just as successfully using stemmed purple sprouting broccoli in place of the asparagus.

20 asparagus spears, ends trimmed

1 tablespoon olive oil

sea salt and freshly ground black pepper

2 hard-boiled eggs

FOR THE DRESSING

juice of 1 lemon

1 tablespoon finely chopped shallot

1 tablespoon torn basil leaves

1 teaspoon Dijon mustard

⅛ teaspoon freshly ground black pepper

⅓ cup extra virgin olive oil

Preheat the oven to 350°F.

Toss the asparagus spears in the olive oil and season with salt and pepper. Place on a baking sheet and bake for 10 minutes, or roast on a hot ridged grill pan over high heat for 5 minutes, turning often so that they are evenly cooked.

For the dressing, whisk the lemon juice, shallot, basil, and mustard together in a small bowl and season with salt and the pepper. Then add the extra virgin olive oil in a slow stream, whisking constantly.

Shell and halve the eggs, then push through a medium-mesh sieve into another small bowl or finely chop.

Toss the baked or roasted asparagus with 1 tablespoon of the dressing in a large bowl, then divide the dressed asparagus between four plates. Spoon the remaining dressing over the asparagus and sprinkle the sieved or chopped egg on top.

Watercress Soup with Rosemary & Toasted Pine Nuts

SERVES 4

There is something so decadent about watercress soup. The first time I made it was when I was a chef many years ago at Ballymaloe House in Ireland. When I forage for watercress, I always soak it in a basin of water with lemon juice added after picking to ensure it's thoroughly clean, but you can always just pick some up at your grocery store. The toasted pine nuts add a delicious sweet and nutty flavor, but leave them out if you want a pure watercress soup.

3 tablespoons butter

2¼ cups potatoes, peeled and diced

1 onion, diced

3½ cups hot chicken or vegetable stock

5½ ounces watercress, plus 12 sprigs to garnish, thoroughly washed

½ teaspoon freshly grated nutmeg

sea salt and freshly ground black pepper

½ cup crème fraîche

FOR THE TOPPING

½ cup pine nuts, toasted

1 tablespoon finely chopped rosemary leaves

1 tablespoon crème fraîche

Place a heavy-bottomed saucepan over medium heat and add the butter. Once the butter has melted, add the potatoes and onion, stir well, and cover the pan with a lid. Reduce the heat to low and leave the vegetables to sweat for about 10 minutes, stirring occasionally.

Pour in the hot stock, increase the heat to high, and cook, uncovered, for about 10 minutes until the potatoes and onion are completely soft.

Stir in the watercress and nutmeg and cook for another 5 minutes until the watercress has wilted.

Transfer the soup to a blender or food processor, or use an immersion blender, and process to a smooth consistency.

Return the soup to the saucepan (if necessary) and season with salt and pepper. Stir in the crème fraîche and place over medium heat for just 2 minutes to warm through.

Meanwhile, for the topping, mix the pine nuts, rosemary, and crème fraîche together in a small bowl.

Serve the soup in warmed bowls, topped with a little of the pine nut mixture and the watercress sprigs to garnish.

Dublin Bay Prawn Ceviche

SERVES 4

I made this appetizer for a supper I was hosting at chef Mark Hix's Kitchen Library in East London. The supper was a tastescape around Ireland, and this was my Dublin dish. Dublin Bay prawns (langoustines) are plump and juicy, so they work really well as a ceviche, but you can also use fish, such as fresh tuna, sea bass, flounder, and so on. Don't leave the seafood to marinate for longer than an hour, otherwise it will lose its fresh rawness. Keep the prawn shells for making a bisque—roast them first and then blend them in a power blender with stock and herbs.

16 raw Dublin Bay prawns (langoustines) or other fresh fish

juice of 2 lemons

2 tablespoons olive oil

1 small bunch of wild garlic leaves, thoroughly washed and finely chopped

2 scallions, very finely sliced

1 teaspoon dried red pepper flakes

sea salt

wild garlic flowers, thoroughly washed, to garnish

Remove the heads and shells from the Dublin Bay prawns. Cut into the flesh of each prawn down the back and pull out and discard the black vein that lies just below the surface. This is actually the prawn's digestive tract and needs to be removed. Rinse the prawns briefly in cold water.

Thinly slice the prawns lengthwise, gently pressing your fingers onto the prawns while you cut—this will make it easier to cut thin slices. Divide the thinly sliced prawns between four plates and spread them out so that they cover the whole plate.

For the dressing, whisk the lemon juice, olive oil, wild garlic leaves, scallions, red pepper flakes, and a good seasoning of salt together in a small bowl. Pour the dressing over the prawns. Cover and leave in the fridge for an hour.

Serve straight from the fridge, sprinkled with wild garlic flowers to garnish.

Spring Pea, Pea Shoot, Pancetta & Goat Cheese Salad

SERVES 4

This has to be the prettiest spring salad ever! The delicate peppery taste of the pea shoots alongside the crispy, smoky pancetta, sweet peas, and creamy goat cheese is divine—or try using watercress instead. The dressing, lightly scented with orange, is my favorite with this salad, but if you are fonder of a lemon dressing, then simply replace the orange with a lemon. I recommend doubling up the dressing recipe, as it will last for up to two weeks in the fridge.

1 tablespoon olive oil

¾ cup diced pancetta

7 ounces pea shoots

1½ cups freshly podded peas

¾ cup goat cheese, crumbled

FOR THE DRESSING

½ cup extra virgin olive oil

grated zest and juice of 1 orange

1 teaspoon Dijon mustard

sea salt and freshly ground black pepper

Place a frying pan over medium–high heat and add the olive oil, followed by the pancetta. Cook the pancetta for about 8 minutes until crispy.

Meanwhile, add all the ingredients for the dressing to a bowl and whisk together well. Season with salt and pepper.

Combine all the remaining ingredients for the salad in a large bowl. Drizzle with the dressing, add the crispy pancetta, and gently toss together.

Divide the salad between four plates and serve.

Salt-baked Potato with Crème Fraîche & Trout Caviar

SERVES 4

One of my all-time favorite dishes to make, this combination of hot, fluffy potato filling with silky crème fraîche and peppery flat-leaf parsley, topped with jewels of trout caviar and held within a crispy potato skin, is utterly delicious! I first came up with this recipe when I was curating an Irish menu for Fortnum & Mason in London, and for me it sings of Ireland and it's oh so beautiful... I often make it for a cozy fireside supper on a Friday with a delicious glass of white Burgundy—utter heaven.

4 small Russet potatoes, unpeeled and washed

sea salt and freshly ground black pepper

2 tablespoons chopped flat-leaf parsley

¾ cup crème fraîche

1 tablespoon canola oil

1½ ounces trout caviar

Preheat the oven to 400°F.

Place the potatoes on a baking sheet and bake for 40 minutes.

Remove the baked potatoes from the oven and set aside until cool enough to handle, then cut them in half lengthwise and scoop out the potato flesh into a bowl, leaving the skins intact.

Season the potato flesh with salt and pepper, mash with a fork, and then mix in the parsley and ½ cup of the crème fraîche. Spoon the potato mixture back into the potato skins, place on the baking sheet, and brush the skins with the canola oil so that they crisp.

Bake for 15 minutes until the filling is heated through and the skins are crispy.

Remove the filled potato skins from the oven and spoon the remaining crème fraîche on top, followed by a spoonful of the trout caviar. Serve.

Soft-boiled Egg with Crumbled Blood Sausage & Asparagus

SERVES 2

These are so simple and fast to make. If it's a chilly spring evening, there is nothing better than to cuddle up for supper in front of the fire and devour these delicious gooey eggs using the asparagus spears to dip into the yolks. The blood sausage adds a lovely crumbly texture and spicy flavor, but you can leave it out if you're not a fan and add shavings of Parmesan cheese or crumbles of goat cheese instead.

2 organic or free-range eggs

1 tablespoon olive oil

6 asparagus spears, ends trimmed

sea salt and freshly ground black pepper

1½ ounces blood sausage

For runny yolks, cook the eggs in a saucepan of boiling water over high heat for 5½ minutes.

While the eggs are cooking, place a grill pan over medium–high heat and add the olive oil. Place the asparagus spears on the grill pan and season with salt and pepper, then place the blood sausage alongside. Cook both for 5 minutes, turning the spears often so that they are evenly cooked, and the blood sausage once to cook on both sides.

Once the egg-cooking time is up, immediately transfer the eggs to egg cups or ramekins. Lightly tap the eggs and remove the tops. Season with salt and pepper, then crumble the blood sausage on top of the eggs. Place the egg cups on a plate and arrange the grilled asparagus spears alongside for dipping into the runny yolks.

Watercress Buttered Chicken with Fava Beans & Rosemary Potatoes

SERVES 4

4 chicken supremes (skin-on chicken breasts with the wing bone attached)

FOR THE WATERCRESS BUTTER

2½ cups watercress, chopped, plus extra sprigs to garnish

7 tablespoons butter, softened

sea salt and freshly ground black pepper

FOR THE ROSEMARY POTATOES

2¼ pounds potatoes, sliced

2 tablespoons chopped rosemary leaves

2 garlic cloves, crushed

2 tablespoons olive oil

FOR THE FAVA BEANS

2½ cups fresh fava beans

1 tablespoon olive oil

grated zest and juice of 1 lemon

2 tablespoons chopped mint

Watercress has such a lovely peppery but delicate flavor, so it's delicious with chicken and alongside minted fava beans. I also use this recipe for roasting a whole chicken when I want a more relaxed supper, and I place the fava beans and potatoes in warmed serving bowls and let everyone help themselves. When I am making the watercress butter, I make a big batch, then roll it into a long sausage shape, wrap it in plastic wrap, and freeze it for slicing and topping other dishes like broiled fish or steamed potatoes.

Preheat the oven to 400°F.

To make the watercress butter, add the chopped watercress and the butter to a bowl and season with salt and pepper, then mix together well—I find using the back of a spoon is the best way to blend the ingredients together.

Smear the watercress butter all over the chicken supremes, working it under the skin of the chicken, too. Place a grill pan or frying pan over medium–high heat, add the chicken supremes, and brown on each side. Transfer to a roasting pan and roast for 25 minutes.

While the chicken is roasting, blanch the sliced potatoes in a saucepan half-filled with water over high heat for 10 minutes, then drain and transfer to a bowl. Add the rosemary, garlic, and olive oil, season with salt and pepper, and toss well. Place a frying pan over medium heat, add the potatoes, and fry, tossing every couple of minutes, for about 10 minutes until they are cooked through and a lovely golden color.

Finally, cook the fava beans: Bring a saucepan of water to a boil over high heat. Season the water with salt, stir in the fava beans, and cook for just 1 minute or until they float to the surface of the water. Drain and toss with the olive oil, lemon zest and juice, and mint.

Serve the chicken supremes on warmed plates along with the rosemary potatoes and fava beans, garnished with extra watercress sprigs.

Roast Butterflied Lamb with Salsa Verde

SERVES 8

Butterflied and boned is the fastest and easiest way to roast a leg of lamb, and if you aren't great at carving, you will really love the fact that this roast requires slicing rather than carving. If you would prefer a classic mint sauce to the salsa verde, it's also so simple to make. Whisk together 1 cup chopped mint, 1 teaspoon of superfine sugar, 1 tablespoon of hot water, and 2 tablespoons of white wine vinegar and set aside for 20 minutes for the flavors to infuse.

3 tablespoons olive oil

2 tablespoons red wine vinegar

3 garlic cloves, finely sliced

2 tablespoons finely chopped rosemary leaves

sea salt and freshly ground black pepper

3¼-pound boned and butterflied leg of lamb

FOR THE SALSA VERDE

1 tablespoon white wine vinegar

4 basil sprigs, chopped

2 flat-leaf parsley sprigs, chopped

2 garlic cloves, crushed

2 anchovy fillets, chopped

2 tablespoons capers

¾ cup extra virgin olive oil

Preheat the oven to 425°F.

For the marinade, add the olive oil, red wine vinegar, garlic, and rosemary to a small bowl, season with salt and pepper, and mix together well.

Place the lamb, skin-side up, in a roasting pan and pour over the marinade. Using clean hands, rub the marinade into the lamb and then leave it to sit for 30 minutes. This allows the flavors to be absorbed into the lamb and also gives the meat time to come to room temperature before roasting.

When the 30 minutes is up, roast the marinated lamb for 40 minutes.

While the lamb is roasting, add all the ingredients for the salsa verde to a bowl and mix together well.

Remove the roasted lamb from the oven, cover with a loose tent of foil, and let rest for 15 minutes.

Thinly slice the roasted lamb onto a warmed platter and spoon the salsa verde down the center of the lamb. Serve.

Wild Garlic Tagliatelle with Goat Cheese, Zucchini & Toasted Almonds

SERVES 4

I love making this dish during the spring because it's so light and fragrant. During the remainder of the year, I simply replace the wild garlic with other fresh herbs that are in season, such as basil, mint, or oregano. I sometimes add grilled fish, shrimp, or chicken to this dish for a weekday one-course supper.

2 tablespoons olive oil

4 zucchini, cut into ribbons using a vegetable peeler

sea salt and freshly ground black pepper

18 ounces fresh tagliatelle

¼ cup chopped wild garlic leaves

¾ cup goat cheese

1 cup blanched almonds, toasted and chopped

½ cup Parmesan cheese, shaved

Place a grill pan or frying pan over medium–high heat and add 1 tablespoon of the olive oil. Add the zucchini ribbons to the pan and cook for 2 minutes on each side. Season with salt and pepper.

Meanwhile, bring a large saucepan of salted water to a boil over high heat. Stir in the fresh pasta and cook for 3 minutes. Drain the cooked pasta and return to the pan, then add the remaining tablespoon of olive oil and gently toss to coat.

Stir the wild garlic, grilled zucchini ribbons, goat cheese, and almonds into the pasta, and season with salt and pepper.

Serve the tagliatelle on a warmed platter or individual plates with the Parmesan shavings sprinkled on top.

Sea Bream & Clams with Purple Sprouting Broccoli, Romesco & Crunchy Seeds

SERVES 4

4 sea bream fillets (skin on), or substitute salmon, sea bass, or mackerel

1 tablespoon olive oil

sea salt and freshly ground black pepper

12 heads of purple sprouting broccoli

9 ounces live clams, rinsed under cold running water (discard any with damaged shells or open shells that won't close when tapped)

10 cherry tomatoes, halved

2 garlic cloves, thinly sliced

2 teaspoons thyme leaves, chopped

½ cup dry white wine

¼ cup mixed pumpkin and sunflower seeds

FOR THE ROMESCO SAUCE

1 large roasted red bell pepper from a jar

1 garlic clove, smashed

½ cup blanched almonds, toasted

¼ cup tomato purée

2 tablespoons chopped flat-leaf parsley

2 tablespoons sherry vinegar

1 teaspoon smoked paprika

½ teaspoon cayenne pepper

½ cup extra virgin olive oil

I love cooking fish for supper, and it's probably my favorite choice because I grew up on the island of Ireland where you can get some of the best fish in the world. I vary the types of fish I use in this dish—anything that's in season and quite meaty with a skin that will crisp up, such as salmon, sea bass, or mackerel. The romesco sauce is fantastic and I would urge you to learn this recipe by heart, as you can use it as a dip or drizzled over grilled asparagus as an appetizer or in a pasta dish. Serve with a big leafy green salad.

Preheat the oven to 400°F.

Place the sea bream fillets, skin-side up, on a baking sheet. Brush with the olive oil and season with salt and pepper. Roast for 15 minutes.

While the fish is cooking, make the romesco sauce: Add all the ingredients to a food processor and process to a thick consistency. Transfer the sauce to a bowl and set aside.

Cook the broccoli in a small quantity of water in a saucepan over medium heat for about 5–6 minutes until al dente (or longer if you prefer not to have a bite in your stalk), then drain.

Meanwhile, place the clams in another saucepan with the cherry tomatoes, garlic, thyme, and wine and cook over high heat for 10 minutes or until the clams open (discard any that remain closed).

Divide the clams and their cooking juice between four warmed plates and place the roasted sea bream on top. Next, place the cooked broccoli in a warmed serving dish, spoon the romesco sauce on top, sprinkle with the pumpkin and sunflower seeds, then serve.

Soda-breaded Pork Chops with Irish Honey & Whiskey Dip & Colcannon

SERVES 4

FOR THE COLCANNON

2¼ pounds potatoes, unpeeled and washed

½ cup milk

4 spring onions or 3½ ounces cabbage, finely chopped

3 tablespoons butter

¼ teaspoon freshly grated nutmeg

FOR THE BREADING

2 garlic cloves, crushed

2 small shallots, finely chopped

1¾ cups fresh soda bread crumbs

2 tablespoons Dijon mustard

1 teaspoon thyme leaves

sea salt and freshly ground black pepper

½ cup all-purpose flour

2 eggs, beaten

4 French-trimmed pork chops on the bone

3 tablespoons butter

FOR THE IRISH HONEY & WHISKEY DIP

½ cup Irish (or locally sourced) honey

½ cup cider vinegar

½ cup brown sugar

2 tablespoons Dijon mustard

½ cup Irish whiskey

I made this dish a few years back for a party I was hosting at Soho House in New York to celebrate St. Patrick's Day. For me, it's real comfort food, as I grew up in Ireland, and pork chops with colcannon were a staple at home. You can use regular fresh white bread crumbs if you don't have soda bread.

Begin preparing the colcannon: Place the whole potatoes in a large saucepan, with the largest ones at the bottom, and fill the pan halfway with water. Cover the pan with a lid and place over high heat. When the water begins to boil, drain off about half so that there is just enough left in the pan for the potatoes to steam. Leave to steam, covered, for 30–40 minutes, depending on the size of the potatoes, until soft. Preheat the oven to 400°F.

To make the breading, add the garlic, shallots, bread crumbs, mustard, and thyme leaves to a food processor. Season with salt and pepper and process for 30 seconds. Transfer the mustard bread crumb mixture to a bowl. Place the flour and beaten eggs in two separate bowls (or on plates). Dip each pork chop in the flour, followed by the beaten egg, then turn in the mustard bread crumb mixture to coat.

Heat an ovenproof frying pan over high heat and add the butter. Once the butter has melted, place the breaded chops in the pan and brown on each side, then transfer the pan to the oven and cook for 20 minutes.

While the potatoes finish cooking, pour the milk for the colcannon into a saucepan and place over medium heat. Stir in the spring onions or cabbage, butter, and nutmeg, season with salt and pepper, and simmer for 4 minutes.

Once the potatoes are cooked, hold them in a kitchen towel while you peel them and place in a warmed bowl. Mash the potatoes while you gradually add the warm milk and spring onion or cabbage mixture.

To make the dip, whisk the honey, vinegar, and sugar together in a bowl until smooth. Transfer to a saucepan and place over medium-high heat, stirring constantly to prevent burning, until the mixture begins to boil and thicken. Whisk in the mustard and whiskey and cook for another minute, continuing to stir constantly. Remove the pan from the heat.

Spoon the colcannon around a large warmed platter, place the breaded pork chops in the center, then pour the honey and whiskey dip over the chops.

Hazelnut & Herb-crusted Lamb Cutlets with Pea & Wild Garlic Purée

SERVES 6

The flavors of the herbs and hazelnuts roasted along with the lamb cutlets are utter heaven here, but you could use almonds or pine nuts instead if you prefer. The last time I made this dish was at my good friend and London theater queen Sally Greene's house. Since it was a large supper gathering, I prepared the pea and wild garlic purée ahead in the morning, along with the lamb cutlets right up to the stage of putting them in the oven, so it was very easy to serve. My pan-fried Rosemary Potatoes (see page 39) make a delicious accompaniment.

3 French-trimmed racks of lamb (about 6 cutlets per rack)

2 tablespoons finely chopped mixed rosemary, thyme, and flat-leaf parsley

¾ cup blanched hazelnuts, toasted and crushed (see page 156)

2 tablespoons olive oil

FOR THE PEA & WILD GARLIC PURÉE

4½ cups frozen peas

3 ounces wild garlic leaves, thoroughly washed and chopped

5 tablespoons salted butter

sea salt and freshly ground black pepper

wild garlic flowers and pert leaves, thoroughly washed, to garnish

Remove the racks of lamb from the fridge at least 30 minutes before cooking.

Preheat the oven to 350°F.

Using a sharp knife, score the fat of the lamb racks in a crisscross pattern. Heat a large frying pan over high heat. Add each rack in turn, fat side down, to the hot pan and sear the fat, then transfer to a large roasting pan.

Mix the herbs, hazelnuts, and olive oil together in a small bowl, then press the mixture onto the seared fat of the lamb racks. Roast for 15 minutes.

While the lamb is roasting, prepare the pea and wild garlic purée: Cook the frozen peas in a saucepan of boiling water for 4 minutes. Drain and add to a blender or food processor along with the wild garlic and butter. Season with salt and pepper and blend to a smooth consistency. Transfer the purée to a saucepan ready to warm through just before serving.

Remove the lamb racks from the oven and let rest for 5 minutes, then slice into individual cutlets. Spoon the warmed pea and wild garlic purée in the center of four warmed plates and lay three lamb cutlets on top. Garnish each serving with wild garlic flowers and a pert wild garlic leaf.

Lobster Linguine

This is my go-to supper dish for two, when I feel like serving something a little special that doesn't take much time to prepare but still has incredible flavors. When I don't want to splash out on lobster I use langoustines, shrimp, or mussels instead—all are equally delicious!

9 ounces dried linguine

7 tablespoons unsalted butter

2 shallots, finely diced

1 teaspoon dried red pepper flakes

2 garlic cloves, crushed

¼ cup dry white wine

7-ounce can cherry tomatoes

sea salt and freshly ground black pepper

2 lobster tails, freshly cooked, shelled, and chopped

1 tablespoon chopped flat-leaf parsley

Bring a large saucepan of salted water to a boil over high heat. Stir in the linguine and keep stirring for the first 2 minutes of cooking—this will keep the pasta from sticking together. Continue to cook the pasta according to the package instructions until al dente. Drain the pasta, reserving a few tablespoons of the cooking water. Return the cooked pasta to the pan, adding the reserved pasta cooking water to prevent it from clumping together.

While the pasta is cooking, place a frying pan over medium heat and add the butter. Once the butter is melted, stir in the shallots, red pepper flakes, and garlic and let cook for about a minute.

Add the white wine and cook for about 2 minutes until the alcohol has evaporated. Stir in the canned cherry tomatoes, season with salt and pepper, and cook for 1 minute. Then add the chopped lobster meat and parsley and warm through.

Place the saucepan with the pasta over low heat, stir in the lobster sauce, and continue to stir until all the sauce has coated the pasta before serving.

Coconut & Lemon Cloud Cake

MAKES I CAKE

A beautifully light, fluffy cake scented with the exotic flavor of coconut and fresh, citrusy lemon, this is the perfect finale for a pungent wild garlic supper to cleanse the palate, although it works equally well as an afternoon treat. You can use coconut butter instead of dairy butter and/or coconut flour in place of the wheat flour. And for convenience, you can make and bake the cake layers a couple of days ahead and then prepare the frosting and assemble the cake on the day you are planning to serve it.

FOR THE CAKE

2½ cups all-purpose flour

I teaspoon baking powder

I teaspoon baking soda

1½ cups superfine sugar

2 sticks + 5 tablespoons unsalted butter, melted, plus extra for greasing

I cup coconut milk

2 eggs

juice of I lemon

I tablespoon coconut oil

I teaspoon vanilla extract

FOR THE FROSTING

I stick + 6 tablespoons unsalted butter, softened

2 cups confectioners' sugar, sifted

grated zest and juice of I lemon

I teaspoon coconut oil

2 cups raw coconut flakes, to decorate

Preheat the oven to 350°F and lightly grease two 8-inch loose-bottomed sandwich pans.

For the cake, sift the flour, baking powder, and baking soda into a large bowl or the bowl of a stand mixer fitted with the paddle attachment and mix in the sugar. In a separate bowl, combine the melted butter, coconut milk, eggs, lemon juice, coconut oil, and vanilla extract and whisk together thoroughly. Add the wet mixture to the dry mixture and beat together until well-combined.

Divide the cake batter evenly between the prepared pans and level the surface with a spatula or the back of a spoon. Bake for about 25 minutes or until well-risen and golden.

Remove the cakes from the oven and let cool in the pans for about 15 minutes, then remove them from the pans and transfer to a wire rack to cool completely.

To make the frosting, place all the ingredients in a bowl or the bowl of the stand mixer and use an electric hand mixer or the paddle attachment on the stand mixer to beat on high speed until light and fluffy.

To assemble, place one of the cakes, top facing downward, on a cake plate or stand and spread with about one-third of the frosting to cover it. Add the other cake, top facing upward, and cover the entire cake with the remaining frosting. Sprinkle raw coconut flakes all over the cake to decorate.

Rhubarb, Rosewater & Pistachio Galettes

FOR THE FILLING

1¼ pounds rhubarb, trimmed and cut diagonally into 1-inch pieces

½ cup superfine sugar

2 tablespoons rosewater

FOR THE DOUGH

1½ cups all-purpose flour, plus extra for dusting

1 stick + 2 tablespoons unsalted butter, chilled and cubed

1 tablespoon superfine sugar

2 tablespoons cold water

FOR GLAZING

1 egg

1 tablespoon milk

1 tablespoon brown sugar

FOR THE PISTACHIO ROSEWATER MASCARPONE

⅓ cup pistachio nuts, chopped

½ cup mascarpone cheese

1 tablespoon rosewater

Rosewater, one of my favorite flavors, is delicately fragrant, and I suggest buying a bottle or two for your pantry. Whenever I am roasting rhubarb I add a few dashes of rosewater, but it's also delicious added to whipped cream, sponge cakes, raspberries, strawberries—I could go on...

These galettes are so easy to make. Once you have prepared the dough, it really is only a matter of spooning the rhubarb in the center and popping them in the oven. At other times of the year you can substitute whichever fruits are in season, such as apples or peaches, for the rhubarb. Last Easter I made one large version of the galette and it looked amazing on the table.

For the filling, place the rhubarb in a bowl with the superfine sugar and toss well to coat the rhubarb. Transfer the rhubarb to a colander set over a bowl and leave for a couple of hours to release any excess moisture.

To make the dough, place the flour, butter, and sugar in a food processor and pulse until you have a bread crumb consistency. Transfer the mixture to a large bowl and drizzle with the cold water. Gently mix with your hands until a dough forms. Turn the dough onto a lightly floured work surface and knead it together, pressing to incorporate any dry bits of flour. Flatten the dough into a disk about 1-inch thick, wrap in plastic wrap, and chill in the refrigerator for at least an hour.

Preheat the oven to 350°F. Line a baking sheet with parchment paper.

Transfer the rhubarb to a bowl, add the rosewater, and toss to combine. In a small bowl, beat the egg and milk for glazing together. Set both aside while you roll out the dough.

Remove the dough from the fridge, unwrap, and cut it into four equal pieces. Roll out one piece of dough on a lightly floured work surface into a 5-inch round. Spoon one-quarter of the rhubarb filling into the center of the round, leaving a 5-inch border. Brush the border with the egg wash and fold the edges of the dough up and over the rhubarb, overlapping slightly. Brush the border with the egg wash and sprinkle with a little of the brown sugar. Repeat the process to make the other galettes and transfer them to the lined baking sheet.

Bake for 35–40 minutes until the dough is golden brown.

For the mascarpone, mix the pistachios, mascarpone, and rosewater together in a small bowl and serve alongside the warm baked galettes.

Guinness Caramel Tiramisu

SERVES 4

Ever since living in Italy a few years back, I have a real soft spot for tiramisu. The Guinness caramel brings a fun twist to the original recipe as well as a delicious depth of flavor, and makes it a great Irish dessert to serve on St. Patrick's Day. You can always leave out the Guinness if you prefer, or skip the caramel completely for a classic tiramisu.

I like to make my tiramisu in individual vintage cocktail glasses, but you could easily double up the recipe and make it in a glass trifle bowl for a spectacular centerpiece. This is a dessert that you can make ahead the night before.

3 egg yolks

½ cup superfine sugar

1¾ cups mascarpone cheese

14 Savoiardi ladyfingers

½ cup cold strong coffee or espresso

1⅓ cups cocoa powder

FOR THE GUINNESS CARAMEL

¾ cup superfine sugar

½ cup water

4 tablespoons unsalted butter

½ cup half-and-half

½ cup Guinness

Place the egg yolks and superfine sugar in a large bowl and use a hand blender to whisk together until pale and thick. Add the mascarpone and whisk slowly until the mixture is pale and smooth.

To make the Guinness caramel, add the sugar and water to a saucepan, place over low heat, and stir until the sugar has dissolved. Increase the heat to high and cook for 12–14 minutes, or until the syrup is light golden brown in color. Stir in the butter and cook for another 2–3 minutes or until the mixture is a caramel consistency. Stir in the cream and Guinness, then reduce the heat and simmer for 10 minutes, or until the caramel is a thick consistency.

Dip the ladyfingers into the cold coffee and then place straight into four cocktail glasses to create the base layer. Alternatively, arrange the coffee-dipped ladyfingers in a large glass bowl to make one large tiramisu.

Spoon half the mascarpone mixture over the ladyfingers, followed by a layer of the Guinness caramel and a sprinkle of cocoa, and then another layer of the remaining mascarpone mixture and Guinness caramel. Finish with a layer of cocoa on top.

Cover and chill for an hour before serving.

Rhubarb & Crystallized Ginger Upside-down Cake

MAKES 1 CAKE

This cake is one of the easiest to make. It's similar to a tarte tatin in that you caramelize the rhubarb first in an ovenproof frying pan, then pour the batter over and transfer directly to the oven to bake—simple as that! I add crystallized ginger both to the batter and the rhubarb, as it's one of my favorite ingredients and it brings a fantastic sweet yet tangy bite to the cake. You can use other fruits according to the season, such as apples, peaches, and pears.

3 tablespoons unsalted butter

1 cup brown sugar

2 tablespoons finely chopped crystallized ginger

¾ pound rhubarb, trimmed and cut into ¾-inch pieces

1½ cups all-purpose flour

1 teaspoon baking powder

¼ teaspoon baking soda

¾ cup buttermilk

2 eggs

½ cup vegetable oil

crème fraîche, to serve

Preheat the oven to 350°F.

Melt the butter in a 10-inch ovenproof frying pan over medium heat. Stir in half the sugar and cook for about 2 minutes, then stir in one-third of the crystallized ginger. Remove the pan from the heat and add the rhubarb pieces to cover the bottom of the pan.

Sift the flour, baking powder, and baking soda into a bowl.

In a separate bowl, whisk the remaining sugar with the buttermilk, eggs, oil, and the remaining crystallized ginger. Fold in the flour mixture and mix well. Pour the batter over the rhubarb and level the surface with a spatula or the back of a spoon.

Bake for 30 minutes or until the cake springs back when you press it in the center with your fingertip.

Remove the cake from the oven and let cool in the pan on a wire rack for 10 minutes, then invert onto a serving plate and serve with crème fraîche.

Lemon Verbena Possets

SERVES 4

I had kind of forgotten about possets until recently when I was at my favorite Italian restaurant in London, Trullo. They had lemon posset on the dessert menu, which I ordered, served with buttery shortbread for scooping into the posset. It reminded me just how good a posset can be. This recipe is the closest I have come to capturing the Trullo moment. I have added lemon verbena, as it gives it such a delicious lemon depth, but don't worry if you can't find it because you can just leave it out. You can make this dessert up to two days before serving, keeping it in the fridge.

2 lemons

½ cup superfine sugar

6 lemon verbena leaves, plus 4 leaves to serve

1¾ cups heavy cream

Grate the zest of the lemons into a saucepan, then squeeze out and add the juice, followed by the sugar and lemon verbena leaves.

Place the pan over low heat and bring to a boil, stirring occasionally until the sugar has dissolved. Whisk in the cream and cook for 3 minutes.

Divide the mixture between four small glasses or ramekins. Let cool, then chill in the fridge for 2 hours until set.

Remove the possets from the fridge at least 30 minutes before serving and top each posset with a lemon verbena leaf before serving.

My Italian Baked Ricotta Cheesecake

MAKES 1 CHEESECAKE

I used to make this dessert every couple of weeks when I lived in Northern Italy, on a square called Piazza Madama Cristina, where there was a daily market that sold the most fantastic lemons from Amalfi. Every time I make it, it takes me back to sunny mornings waking up in my apartment and having an espresso on my balcony while watching all the farmers and vendors setting up their stalls.

I love the savory sweetness of this baked cheesecake, which is wonderful served with a dollop of crème fraîche scented with lemon zest. When I make it in the summer, I poach summer berries in sugar syrup to serve over the cake. You can prepare and bake the cheesecake up to two days before serving it, keeping it refrigerated in the meantime.

1½ cups ricotta cheese

4 eggs, separated

2 tablespoons all-purpose flour

grated zest and juice of 2 lemons

1 cup superfine sugar

5 tablespoons butter

1½ cups graham cracker crumbs

¾ cup pine nuts, toasted and finely chopped

Preheat the oven to 350°F.

Place the ricotta in a bowl and whisk in the egg yolks followed by the flour, lemon zest and juice, and sugar until well-combined.

In a separate, very clean and dry bowl, whisk the egg whites until they are stiff and then fold into the ricotta mixture.

Place a saucepan over low heat and add the butter. Once the butter has melted, remove the pan from the heat and stir in the graham cracker crumbs and chopped pine nuts.

Spoon the crumb mixture into a 10-inch springform cake pan, using the back of the spoon to spread and press it into an even, well-compacted base.

Pour the lemon ricotta mixture over the base, then bake for 55 minutes.

Remove the cheesecake from the oven. Serve at room temperature or chilled.

Lemon Meringue Pie

MAKES 1 PIE

FOR THE DOUGH

1½ cups all-purpose flour, plus extra for dusting

7 tablespoons butter, chilled and cubed

1 tablespoon confectioners' sugar

1 egg yolk (reserve the white for the meringue—see below)

1 tablespoon cold water

FOR THE FILLING

1 tablespoon cornstarch

grated zest and juice of 2 large lemons

½ cup superfine sugar

5 tablespoons butter, diced

3 egg yolks (reserve the whites for the meringue—see below)

1 egg

FOR THE MERINGUE

4 egg whites, at room temperature

¾ cup superfine sugar

1 teaspoon cornstarch

This is my favorite dessert for serving on a Sunday after a big feast of roasted lamb! If you are nervous about making dough, don't be—just put the ingredients in a food processor, pulse, and roll! You can make it a few days in advance when you have the chance and keep it in the fridge, but if you are stretched for time, just buy your dough from the grocery store. The pie is at its best on the day of baking.

First make the dough: Place all the ingredients in a food processor and pulse until combined. Turn the dough onto a lightly floured work surface and knead it together until smooth. Roll out the dough and use to line a 10-inch diameter loose-bottomed fluted flan pan, 1-inch deep. Trim the excess dough around the edges and prick the bottom with a fork. Line the dough with a sheet of foil and chill in the fridge for an hour.

Preheat the oven to 350°F.

Remove the dough from the fridge, pour baking beans on top of the foil, and bake the dough "blind" for 15 minutes. Set aside to cool.

To prepare the filling, mix the cornstarch, lemon zest and juice, and sugar together in a saucepan. Place over medium heat and cook, stirring constantly, until thickened. Remove the pan from the heat and whisk in the butter. Beat the egg yolks and whole egg together in a bowl, then stir into the pan and return it to medium heat. Cook, stirring vigorously for a few minutes until the mixture thickens again, then remove the pan from the heat and set aside.

To make the meringue, place the egg whites in a very clean and dry large bowl (using a stainless steel one will give you a stiffer meringue) or the bowl of a stand mixer and use a hand mixer or the whisk attachment on the stand mixer to whisk until soft peaks form. Gradually add half the sugar, a tablespoon at a time, whisking constantly, then whisk in the cornstarch. Finally, add the remaining sugar and whisk until smooth and stiff.

Reheat the filling and then pour it into the dough base. Immediately add spoonfuls of meringue around the edge of the filling, then spread it so that it just touches the dough side. Pile the remaining meringue into the center of the pie, then spread it so that it touches the surface of the hot filling (and starts to cook). Using a knife, swirl the meringue into soft peaks.

Bake for 18–20 minutes until the meringue is crisp and slightly colored. Remove the pie from the oven and let cool in the pan for 30 minutes, then remove it from the pan and let cool on a wire rack for another 30 minutes–1 hour before slicing.

Summer Suppers

Menus

4TH OF JULY SUPPER

MAPLE & HARISSA CHICKEN WINGS
WITH TABBOULEH

BARBECUED WHISKEY RIBS
WITH SUMMER SLAW

BERRY TRIFLE

BARBECUE PARTY

SMOKY EGGPLANT WITH MINT
& POMEGRANATE DRESSING

BARBECUED ROUND STEAK WITH
CHIMICHURRI & CHARRED CHICORY

BARBECUED PEACHES WITH ROSEMARY
& MAPLE BUTTER

EDIBLE FLOWER SUPPER

ZUCCHINI BLOSSOMS FILLED WITH
RICOTTA & IRISH HONEY

DANDELION, SAFFRON & SHEEP
CHEESE RISOTTO

SWEET GERANIUM CHEESECAKE

SUMMER GARDEN SUPPER

GAZPACHO WITH CUCUMBER &
DILL SALSA

LEMON, HARISSA & OLIVE SPATCHCOCK
CHICKEN WITH BULGUR WHEAT,
CUCUMBER & DILL

ORANGE BLOSSOM SUMMER CAKE WITH
CREAM & STRAWBERRIES

SUMMER GATHERING

BEET, BLOOD ORANGE
& GIN-CURED SALMON
WITH FENNEL & DILL PICKLE

SEAFOOD PAELLA

RASPBERRY & ROSEWATER PAVLOVA

FORAGED SUPPER

NETTLE SOUP WITH SEAWEED SCONES

WHOLE BAKED SEA BASS WITH HERBS,
LEMON & BUTTERED PURSLANE

CARRAGEEN MOSS PUDDINGS WITH
CARRAGEEN FRITTERS

WILD SALMON SUPPER

SHRIMP PIL PIL WITH DIPPING TOASTS

WHOLE POACHED WILD SALMON
WITH FRESH HORSERADISH CREAM
& NEW POTATO SALAD

WATERMELON & MINT GRANITA

Nettle Soup with Seaweed Scones

SERVES 4

3 tablespoons butter

2¼ cups potatoes, peeled and diced

1 onion, diced

3½ cups hot vegetable stock

7 ounces young nettle leaves and tender stalks, thoroughly washed

½ teaspoon freshly grated nutmeg

sea salt and freshly ground black pepper

½ cup heavy cream

clover blossoms, thoroughly washed, to garnish

FOR THE SEAWEED SCONES

½ ounce dulse, finely chopped (you could also use other varieties, such as kelp)

1¾ cups all-purpose flour, plus extra for dusting

1 tablespoon baking powder

pinch of fine sea salt

3 tablespoons butter, chilled and cubed

½ cup buttermilk, plus extra for brushing

vegetable oil, for oiling

Nettles grow wild everywhere, so it's easy to forage for them—just wear rubber gloves! Pick the small leaves at the top because they are the sweetest, and fret not—once they are dropped in boiling water they lose their sting. Nettles are incredibly good for you, as they are packed with iron. The taste is similar to spinach, but more interesting and sweeter. The seaweed scones add a delicious saltiness to the dish. If you don't want to use seaweed in the scones, then rosemary, thyme, or dried oregano would be delicious instead.

Place a heavy-bottomed saucepan over medium heat and add the butter. Once the butter has melted, add the potatoes and onion, stir well, and cover the pan with a lid. Reduce the heat to low and leave the vegetables to sweat for about 10 minutes, stirring occasionally.

Pour in the hot stock, increase the heat to high, and cook, uncovered, for about 10 minutes until the potatoes and onion are completely soft.

Using gloves, add the nettles (they lose their sting once cooked) and nutmeg, stir, and cook for 2–3 minutes until the nettles have wilted.

Transfer the soup to a blender or food processor, or use an immersion blender, and blend to a smooth consistency.

Return the soup to the saucepan (if necessary) and season. Stir in the cream and place over medium heat for just 2 minutes to warm through.

Meanwhile, make the scones: Preheat the oven to 400°F.

Spread the dulse out on a baking sheet, roast in the oven for 2 minutes, then remove from the oven.

Sift the flour, baking powder, and salt into a large bowl. Add the butter and rub in with your fingertips until the mixture resembles fine bread crumbs.

Stir the dulse into the mixture, then gradually mix in enough buttermilk with a fork to make a soft dough. Roll out the dough on a floured work surface to a thickness of ½-inch. Cut into rounds using a 3-inch pastry cutter or an upturned glass. Oil the baking sheet used for the dulse, place the rounds on the pan, and brush with buttermilk. Bake for 12–15 minutes until golden brown. Transfer the scones to a wire rack and let cool for 10 minutes before serving.

Serve the soup in warmed bowls, garnished with clover blossoms, along with the warm seaweed scones.

Zucchini Blossoms Filled with Ricotta & Irish Honey

My all-time favorite summer appetizer—crisp blossoms filled with light and creamy honeyed ricotta. I use beautiful wild Irish honey, but you can source a good local honey—it will make a world of difference to the flavor of the dish. I sometimes serve this as a main course with grilled zucchini circled around the plate. The best tip I can pass on for when you are cooking these is to ensure you twist the top of the zucchini blossom and hold onto it as you are dropping each one into the batter and then the oil. This will help keep it from breaking apart when frying. You can get the filling made the day ahead and then fill the zucchini blossoms on the day you plan to cook them.

¾ cup ricotta cheese

2 tablespoons chopped mint

⅓ cup Irish (or locally sourced) honey

12 zucchini flowers

¾ cup vegetable oil

1⅔ cups pea shoots

sea salt

FOR THE BATTER

1 all-purpose flour

2 teaspoons baking soda

1¾ cups soda water

For the filling, beat the ricotta in a bowl until soft and smooth, then stir in the mint and honey. Carefully scoop the filling into the zucchini flowers—you should be able to fit 2–4 teaspoons in each one, depending on their size. Twist the petals gently to enclose the mixture.

Just before you are ready to cook, prepare the batter: Sift the flour and baking soda together into a bowl, then lightly whisk in the soda water until you have a batter with the consistency of half-and-half. Be careful not to overwhisk, so don't worry if there are a few lumps of flour remaining.

Heat the vegetable oil in a deep saucepan to 350–375°F or until a cube of bread browns in 30 seconds.

Dip one stuffed zucchini flower into the batter and immediately lower into the hot oil, then repeat with a couple more—don't cook more than three or four at a time. Deep-fry for 1–2 minutes until puffed up, crisp, and golden brown. Remove from the oil and drain on paper towels while you fry the remaining stuffed flowers. Season with salt.

To serve, arrange the fried zucchini flowers on a plate and sprinkle the pea shoots around them.

Shrimp Pil Pil with Dipping Toasts

SERVES 6

I remember the first time that I ever had shrimp pil pil. It was in the famous Boqueria market in Barcelona. I sat at the counter of one of the tapas bars, and watched how they fired up the plump fresh shrimp with fiery chiles, aromatic garlic, and smoky paprika. They were out of this world... They served them with very thinly sliced sourdough toasts that were brushed with olive oil. I scooped the shrimp pil pil onto the toasts to create the perfect bite! It is one of the easiest and fastest appetizers that I know. I also make them when I want a late-night supper that's light but bursting with flavor.

½ cup olive oil

6 garlic cloves, sliced

1 teaspoon dried red pepper flakes

30 raw shrimp, peeled and deveined

2 teaspoons smoked paprika

1 tablespoon dry sherry

juice of 1 lemon

1 tablespoon chopped flat-leaf parsley

sea salt and freshly ground black pepper

sourdough toasts, to serve

Place a frying pan over medium heat and add the olive oil, followed by the garlic and red pepper flakes. Cook for 2 minutes.

Toss in the shrimp, followed by the smoked paprika, dry sherry, and lemon juice, and season with salt and pepper. Cook for another 2 minutes, or until the shrimp are cooked. Just before you take the pan off the heat, toss in the parsley.

Serve with sourdough toasts for scooping up all the juices.

Smoky Eggplant with Mint & Pomegranate Dressing

SERVES 6

I just love the flavor of smoked eggplant. When I am not using the grill, I smoke the eggplant by placing them over a gas flame, turning every few minutes, to blacken the skin. Do this for about 15 minutes until the eggplant collapses, or grill them on a hot grill pan. The dressing is so delicious with the smoky eggplant, and do sprinkle extra pomegranate seeds and chopped fresh mint on top before you serve to make it pretty.

2 eggplants, sliced

sea salt and freshly ground black pepper

2 tablespoons olive oil

FOR THE MINT & POMEGRANATE DRESSING

¾ cup Greek yogurt

2 tablespoons chopped mint

1 tablespoon tahini

juice of ½ lemon

1 pomegranate

Lay out the eggplant slices and lightly sprinkle the exposed sides with salt, then leave for 10 minutes until you see beads of water come to the surface. Dry the eggplant slices off with paper towels, then turn them over and repeat the process. This keeps the eggplant from tasting bitter.

Prepare a charcoal grill or heat a gas grill to high heat, or place a grill pan over high heat. Brush the eggplant slices with the olive oil and grill on each side for 3 minutes.

Meanwhile, make the dressing: Whisk all the ingredients except the pomegranate together in a bowl and season with salt and pepper. Cut the pomegranate in half and then, holding each half in turn, cut-side down over the dressing bowl, use the back of a wooden spoon to firmly tap the skin side of the pomegranate so that the seeds fall directly into the dressing. Mix the pomegranate seeds into the dressing.

Place the grilled eggplant on a serving platter and drizzle the dressing over the top.

Gazpacho with Cucumber & Dill Salsa

SERVES 6

This is so easy to make because it's really just a case of chopping and blending. The key thing is that you use very ripe tomatoes that are full of flavor. The best way to ripen tomatoes is to place them in a brown paper bag with a banana. It sounds odd but it works! And never store tomatoes in the fridge, as they won't ripen properly. I try to make this soup a day ahead and keep it in my fridge. It should be served very chilled. The cucumber and dill salsa adds great texture, and you could also add some croûtons on top if you wish. When I am having lots of people over for a party, I serve the gazpacho in small glasses.

2¼ pounds very ripe tomatoes, diced

2 or 3 slices of slightly stale crusty white or sourdough bread, torn into pieces

2 red bell peppers, cored, seeded, and diced

1 cucumber, diced

2 scallions, chopped

3 garlic cloves, crushed

2 tablespoons sherry vinegar

¾ cup extra virgin olive oil

sea salt and freshly ground black pepper

FOR THE SALSA

½ cucumber, diced

2 tablespoons chopped dill

2 tablespoons extra virgin olive oil

Place the tomatoes, bread, red bell peppers, cucumber, scallions, garlic, sherry vinegar, and olive oil in a blender or food processor and season with salt and pepper. Blend the ingredients until smooth.

Transfer the mixture to a bowl, cover with plastic wrap, and chill in the fridge for an hour.

To make the salsa, mix all the ingredients together in a bowl.

To serve, pour the gazpacho into bowls and spoon the salsa on top.

Beet, Blood Orange & Gin-cured Salmon with Fennel & Dill Pickle

SERVES 4

I developed this recipe for a theater supper that I was cooking at my friend Sally Greene's house in London. The colors are simply dazzling on the plate and this is a really fabulous first course for when you want to get a head start, as you have to prepare it a couple of days beforehand to allow it to cure. If you can't find blood oranges, then just use regular oranges. If you want to slice it before your guests arrive, ensure you wrap it tight in plastic wrap so that it doesn't dry out.

FOR THE SALMON

10½ ounces salmon fillet

¾ cup peeled raw beets, grated

¼ cup granulated sugar

1 tablespoon sea salt

1 tablespoon finely chopped dill

grated zest and juice of 1 small blood orange

2 tablespoons gin

FOR THE FENNEL & DILL PICKLE

1 fennel bulb

⅓ cup granulated sugar

1 tablespoon finely chopped dill

1 teaspoon sea salt

1 cup cider vinegar

1 blood orange, sliced, to decorate (optional)

Start by preparing the salmon, as you will need to let this cure for a couple of days. Place the salmon, skin-side down, in a dish that's deep enough for it to be submerged in the cure—I find a baking or pie dish is perfect. Add all the remaining ingredients for the salmon to a bowl and mix together well. Spoon over the salmon so that the salmon is submerged in the cure. Cover the dish loosely with two sheets of plastic wrap and sit a heavy weight on top—I use cans of tomatoes or similar canned items. Place in the fridge and leave for two days.

Next, make the fennel and dill pickle: Cut the fennel bulb in half down the center and thinly slice into semicircles. Add to a nonreactive bowl, sprinkle with the sugar, dill, and salt, and pour the vinegar on top. Cover the bowl with plastic wrap and let stand at room temperature for about an hour. Give the pickle a good stir and then let stand for another hour.

Once the salmon has cured for two days, remove from the fridge, scrape off all the cure mixture, and pat the salmon dry with paper towels.

To serve, thinly slice the salmon away from the skin underneath and arrange on a serving plate with slices of blood orange, if you wish, and the fennel and dill pickle in a bowl alongside.

Maple & Harissa Chicken Wings with Tabbouleh

SERVES 6

Sticky, sweet, and spicy chicken wings, scooped up with a fresh tabbouleh—utterly delicious! You can leave out the tabbouleh if you just want to serve the chicken wings as finger food. This is perfect barbecue food, and you can get them marinated a day in advance for an extra depth of flavor and to tenderize the chicken.

¾ cup bulgur wheat or couscous

½ cup boiling water

½ cup maple syrup

6 garlic cloves, crushed

2 tablespoons harissa

sea salt and freshly ground black pepper

3¼ pounds organic or free-range chicken wings, tips removed

1 bunch each of mint, cilantro, and flat-leaf parsley, leaves picked

3½ ounces arugula leaves

2 scallions, thinly sliced lengthwise

1 cucumber, diced

2 teaspoons sumac

juice of 1 lemon

⅓ cup extra virgin olive oil

Prepare a charcoal grill or heat a gas grill to high heat, or preheat the oven to 425°F.

Place the bulgur wheat (or couscous) in a heatproof bowl and pour in the boiling water to cover. Cover the bowl with plastic wrap and let soak for about 20 minutes or until all the water is absorbed, then fluff up with a fork.

Mix the maple syrup, three-quarters of the garlic, 1 tablespoon of the harissa, and a large pinch of salt together in a large bowl. Add the chicken wings and toss to coat in the mixture, then arrange in a single layer on a baking sheet.

Roast on the hot grill or in the oven for 45 minutes or until caramelized and golden and cooked through, turning halfway through, then toss with the remaining tablespoon of harissa.

While the chicken wings are roasting, finish preparing the tabbouleh: Mix the herbs, arugula, scallions, and cucumber with the bulgur wheat.

Whisk the sumac, lemon juice, extra virgin olive oil, and remaining garlic together in a small bowl and season with salt and pepper. Add the dressing to the tabbouleh and toss to coat.

Serve the caramelized wings with the tabbouleh.

Dandelion, Saffron & Sheep Cheese Risotto

SERVES 4

3 tablespoons butter

2 shallots, very finely chopped

2 garlic cloves, crushed

1½ cups Arborio (risotto) rice

½ cup dry white wine

2 cups hot vegetable or chicken stock

½ teaspoon saffron threads

⅔ cup soft crumbly sheep cheese, such as feta, crumbled

¼ cup mascarpone cheese

sea salt and freshly ground black pepper

3 ounces dandelion leaves, thoroughly washed

I developed this recipe a few years back when I was doing a takeover at Cheyne Walk Brasserie in London for the Chelsea Flower Show. Every dish on the menu was infused with beautiful edible flowers so, as you can imagine, it was such an exciting menu to create! The dandelions look so pretty in the risotto, but they are a little bitter, so the addition of the saffron balances out the dish with its smoky sweet flavor. I have also used zucchini flowers in this risotto instead of the dandelions.

Place a saucepan over medium heat and add the butter. When the butter has melted, stir in the shallots and garlic, then cover the pan with a lid, reduce the heat, and leave to sweat for about 2 minutes until the shallots are softened but not browned.

Stir in the rice and toast for about 1 minute until it is dry. Pour in the wine, stir, and cook for about 2 minutes until almost all of it has been absorbed.

Add the hot stock, a ladleful at a time, stirring constantly. Wait until the stock has been fully absorbed before adding the next ladleful. It should take 15–20 minutes for all the stock to be absorbed and the rice to be cooked, but check by tasting as you go.

About 2 minutes before the rice is cooked, stir in the saffron. After another minute, stir in the sheep cheese and mascarpone, then continue to cook for another minute before serving. Season with salt and pepper.

Remove the pan from the heat and stir in the dandelion leaves, then divide the risotto between warmed bowls.

Barbecued Round Steak with Chimichurri & Charred Chicory

SERVES 6

I absolutely love the flavors of chimichurri—it adds a massive burst of freshness, heat, and saltiness to the beef. You can use it with chicken, meaty fish, lamb, pork, or over halloumi. The charred chicory is delicious cooked on the grill, and I also love radicchio cooked the same way. If you are looking for a good salad to go along with this dish, then my Bulgur Wheat Salad on page 80 works perfectly.

FOR THE CHIMICHURRI

1 bunch of flat-leaf parsley, coarsely chopped

¼ cup chopped mint

1 tablespooon chopped thyme leaves

2 garlic cloves, crushed

2 anchovy fillets, chopped

2 green chiles, seeded and sliced

½ cup white wine vinegar

2 tablespoons olive oil

1 tablespoon Irish (or locally sourced) honey

FOR THE STEAK

1¾ pounds round steak in one piece

sea salt and freshly ground black pepper

3 heads of white chicory

good-quality extra virgin olive oil, for drizzling

First make the chimichurri: Add all the ingredients to a food processor and pulse until coarsely chopped. Transfer to a bowl and set aside.

Prepare a charcoal grill or heat a gas grill to high heat, or place a grill pan over high heat. Sprinkle the steak with salt and pepper and grill for 3 minutes on each side for medium-rare. Set aside and keep warm.

Grill the chicory for 1 minute on each side or until golden. Remove from the grill or pan, then drizzle with extra virgin olive oil and season with salt and pepper.

Thinly slice the steak, spoon over the chimichurri, and serve with the grilled chicory.

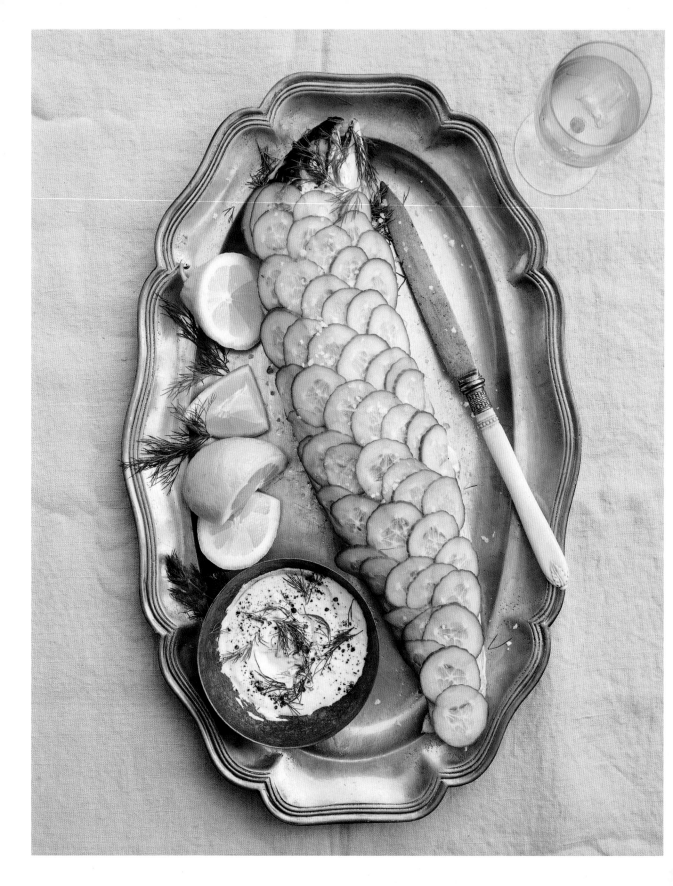

Whole Poached Wild Salmon with Fresh Horseradish Cream & New Potato Salad

SERVES 10

1 whole salmon, about
5½ pounds, scaled and cleaned

3 bay leaves

3 fennel sprigs

2 lemons, cut into wedges

1 teaspoon whole black
peppercorns

½ cucumber

5 fennel sprigs

FOR THE NEW POTATO SALAD

4 pounds new potatoes or
Yukon Golds, washed

6 tablespoons torn mint leaves

sea salt and freshly ground black
pepper

7 tablespoons salted butter

4 shallots, finely diced

grated zest and juice of
2 lemons

2 teaspoons Dijon mustard

40 fresh pea pods, podded, or
1½ cups frozen peas

20 radishes, finely sliced

FOR THE HORSERADISH CREAM

8-inch piece of horseradish root,
peeled and grated

⅔ cup crème fraîche

juice of 1 lemon

The horseradish cream is peppery and utterly delicious with the salmon, but I sometimes serve this with a pistachio yogurt instead—simply mix finely chopped pistachios with plain yogurt and season well. The potato salad is also lovely alongside roasts. Add a couple of tablespoons of crème fraîche if you want a creamier salad, and it's just as good if you make it a day ahead of serving.

Place the salmon in a fish kettle and pour over enough cold water to cover the whole fish. Add the bay leaves, fennel sprigs, half the lemon wedges, and peppercorns. Bring to a boil, then turn off the heat and leave the salmon to cool completely in the water.

For the potato salad, place the potatoes in a saucepan half-filled with water and add 1 tablespoon of the mint and a sprinkle of salt. Cover the pan with a lid and bring to a boil over high heat. Cook for 20–25 minutes or until the potatoes are completely cooked through but still firm.

While the potatoes are cooking, place a frying pan over medium heat and add the butter. Once the butter is melted, add the shallots and cook for about 5 minutes or until soft. Remove the pan from the heat, stir in the lemon zest and juice and mustard, season with salt and pepper, and set aside.

Drain the potatoes, then slice them in half and add them to your serving dish, followed by the fresh peas. If you are using frozen peas, cook them in a pan of salted boiling water for 2–3 minutes, then drain well and add to the potatoes.

Add the radishes, the remaining fresh mint, and the lemon butter to the potatoes. Toss together so all the ingredients are completely coated.

Drain the salmon, leaving it to drain free of any remaining liquid. Using a paring knife or your fingers, carefully remove the skin from the salmon and discard. Transfer the salmon to a serving platter.

For the horseradish cream, add all the ingredients to a small bowl and mix together well.

For the garnish, very thinly slice the cucumber and arrange the slices along the center of the fish. Garnish the rim of the salmon with the fennel sprigs and the remaining lemon wedges and serve with the potato salad and horseradish cream alongside.

Lemon, Harissa & Olive Spatchcock Chicken with Bulgur Wheat, Cucumber & Dill

SERVES 6

Spatchcock chicken is a really great way to get lots of flavors right into the chicken. You can do it yourself or otherwise ask your butcher to do it for you. The combination of the zesty lemons, sweet and smoky harissa, and earthy olive is so Mediterranean. I also use this recipe with meaty fish, like hake or cod. The bulgur wheat is so refreshing and works perfectly alongside the chicken.

1 whole organic or free-range chicken, about 3 pounds

2 preserved lemons, chopped

6 garlic cloves, smashed

½ cup pitted black olives, chopped

1 tablespoon harissa

½ cup olive oil

sea salt and ground black pepper

FOR THE BULGUR WHEAT SALAD

¾ cup bulgur wheat

½ cup boiling water

1 cucumber, diced

4 scallions, thinly sliced

2 tablespoons chopped flat-leaf parsley

2 tablespoons chopped dill

1 tablespoon chopped mint

½ cup extra virgin olive oil

juice of 1 lemon

3 garlic cloves, crushed

Preheat the oven to 350°F.

To spatchcock the chicken, place it breast-side down with the legs toward you. Using sturdy scissors, cut along either side of the backbone to remove it, cutting through the rib bones as you go. Open the chicken out and turn it over. Flatten the breastbone with the heel of your hand so that the meat is all one thickness. You can ask your butcher to do this for you if you prefer.

Add the preserved lemons, garlic, olives, harissa, and olive oil to a bowl and mix together well.

Place the spatchcocked chicken in a roasting pan and rub the preserved lemon and harissa mixture all over the chicken. Season with salt and pepper. Roast for 45 minutes or until cooked through. To check if the chicken is cooked, insert a skewer into the thickest part of the thigh—the juices should run clear.

While the chicken is roasting, prepare the bulgur wheat salad: Place the bulgur in a heatproof bowl and pour in the boiling water to cover. Cover the bowl with plastic wrap and let soak for about 20 minutes or until all the water is absorbed. Fluff up with a fork, then stir in the cucumber, scallions, and herbs. Whisk the oil, lemon juice, and garlic together in a small bowl and season with salt and pepper. Add the dressing to the bulgur wheat salad and toss to coat.

Transfer the roast spatchcocked chicken to the center of a large, warmed platter and spoon the bulgur wheat salad around the chicken to serve.

Whole Baked Sea Bass with Herbs, Lemon & Buttered Purslane

SERVES 4

This is my favorite way to cook and eat fish all year round. Cooking fish on the bone brings so much flavor, and with just a sprinkle of aromatic herbs, zesty lemon juice, and a drizzle of extra virgin olive oil—it's the best way to cook fresh sea bass. Once cooked, sprinkle with fresh herbs, lemon juice, and extra virgin olive oil. I like to serve a large bowl of lightly dressed salad leaves with the fish, as well as the purslane, but nothing too heavy as it should be all about the simple flavors enhancing this beautiful fish. I also love cooking fish like this on the grill.

4 whole sea bass, scaled and cleaned

4 flat-leaf parsley sprigs

4 mint sprigs

4 lemons, sliced, plus 1 for squeezing

sea salt and freshly ground black pepper

3 tablespoons butter

7 ounces purslane, thoroughly washed

¼ cup chopped mixed flat-leaf parsley, mint, and basil

extra virgin olive oil, for drizzling

Preheat the oven to 400°F.

Lay the sea bass on a baking sheet. Add a parsley and mint sprig to the cavity of each fish, along with a sliced lemon. Season with salt and pepper. Bake for 20 minutes.

While the fish finishes baking, place a frying pan over medium heat and add the butter. Once it has melted, add the purslane, season with salt and pepper, and cook, tossing, for 3 minutes.

Remove the sea bass from the oven. Gently lift away and discard the skin, then trim any fat from around the fish. Transfer each fish to a warmed plate. Sprinkle the chopped herbs on top, drizzle with extra virgin olive oil, add a squeeze of lemon, then season with salt and pepper. Serve with the buttered purslane.

Barbecued Whiskey Ribs with Summer Slaw

SERVES 6

4½ pounds pork belly rib racks

FOR THE MARINADE

⅔ cup Irish (or locally sourced) honey

⅔ cup sweet soy sauce

⅔ cup Irish whiskey

4-inch piece of fresh ginger, peeled and grated

1 teaspoon sesame oil

½ teaspoon ground cinnamon

sea salt and freshly ground black pepper

FOR THE SUMMER SLAW

½ cup mayonnaise

2 tablespoons finely chopped flat-leaf parsley

½ green cabbage, cored and cut into strips

2 celery ribs, thinly sliced

2 carrots, peeled and grated

juice of 1 lemon

These ribs are smoky, sweet, and made punchy with the fresh ginger—along with the fresh summer slaw, it's such a fabulous barbecue dish. Get the ribs marinated a day ahead so that they have time to infuse the pork. You can leave the whiskey out of the marinade if you want, and there's no need to replace it with anything. This marinade also works really well with pork chops and chicken pieces. The slaw can also be made the day before so it's all quite stress free!

Whisk all the ingredients for the marinade together in a bowl.

Place the rib racks in a roasting pan and pour over the marinade, turning to coat them all over. Cover loosely with plastic wrap and leave to marinate in the fridge for 4 hours (or overnight if possible).

Preheat the oven to 275°F.

Remove the rib racks from the fridge, uncover, and drain off the excess marinade into a bowl. Baste the ribs with some of the excess marinade, then cover the roasting pan with foil and roast for 4 hours or until the meat is falling off the bone, basting every so often with more marinade.

Remove the roasting pan from the oven and cut the rib racks between the bones into individual ribs. Increase the oven temperature to 425°F, or prepare a charcoal grill or heat a gas grill to high heat.

Meanwhile, to make the summer slaw, toss all the ingredients together in a large serving bowl and season with salt and pepper. Cover the bowl with plastic wrap and leave in the fridge for an hour before serving.

Pour the remaining marinade into a small saucepan and bring to a boil, then reduce the heat and simmer for about 15 minutes until it is syrupy. Paint the ribs with the reduced marinade and return them to the hot oven or grill.

Cook the ribs for about 10 minutes, then turn them over, paint with the remaining reduced marinade, and cook for a final 5–7 minutes until sticky and dark.

Serve the ribs with the summer slaw.

Seafood Paella

SERVES 10

I love serving a seafood paella at home for supper with my friends—one big pan set in the middle of the table for everyone to enjoy. You can make it up to step two a few hours before serving it—just so that you're not chained to the stove when your guests arrive. There are so many alternative fish that you can use instead of the monkfish, the only thing is that they need to be meaty, so fish like hake and cod also work very well. If you don't have any saffron then use 2 teaspoons of smoked paprika. Serve with a big, green leafy salad.

2¼ pounds live mussels

olive oil, for cooking

4-inch piece of fully cured, ready-to-eat chorizo, diced

2 onions, diced

2 red bell peppers, cored, seeded, and sliced

4 garlic cloves, crushed

4 cups paella rice

sea salt and freshly ground black pepper

1 teaspoon saffron threads

4¼ cups hot fish stock

1¼ pounds monkfish fillets, cut into ¾–1¼-inch pieces

10 raw shrimp

2 lemons, cut into wedges, to serve

First prepare the mussels: Rinse them under cold running water, then scrub the shells to remove any barnacles and pull away and discard any stringy beards. Discard any with damaged shells or open shells that won't close when tapped.

Heat a large paella pan over medium heat. Add a splash of olive oil, followed by the chorizo. Cook for about 5 minutes until crisp.

Add the onions, red bell peppers, and garlic to the paella pan and cook for another 10 minutes, stirring frequently.

Stir in the rice and season with salt and pepper. Add the saffron threads and hot stock and leave to simmer for about 15 minutes.

Scatter the pieces of monkfish over the rice and push under the surface with the back of a spoon. Lay the mussels and shrimp over the top and simmer for another 10 minutes or until all the mussels have opened (discard any that remain closed) and the shrimp have turned pink.

Serve the paella in the pan, with the lemon wedges placed around the edge.

Watermelon & Mint Granita

SERVES 6

This is the easiest dessert to make during summer and the most refreshing, but it is also the perfect palate-cleanser to serve after a fish main course. I sometimes use fresh basil instead of the mint, which adds a delicious sweetness.

1 medium watermelon, about 6½ pounds

juice of ½ lemon

½ cup confectioners' sugar, sifted

2 tablespoons finely chopped mint leaves

Cut the melon into wedges, then scrape out the seeds with a teaspoon.

Scoop the pink watermelon flesh into a food processor and pulse until you have a slush. Transfer the watermelon slush to a fine sieve over a bowl and push it through the sieve using the back of a spoon to create the juice.

Whisk the lemon juice and confectioners' sugar into the watermelon juice, then stir in the mint.

Pour the watermelon mixture into a baking sheet or shallow baking pan and place in the freezer. After 30 minutes, remove from the freezer and stir well. Return to the freezer and repeat the process about three more times or until the granita has frozen—about 2 hours in total.

Scoop the granita into chilled glasses to serve.

Raspberry & Rosewater Pavlova

MAKES I PAVLOVA

This is my all-time favorite summer dessert! It is so decadent in flavor and looks absolutely fabulous—everyone loves it! I love the flavor of rosewater and its gentle floral taste works perfectly with the light and fluffy pavlova. I also make the pavlova the evening before and let it cool overnight in the oven (after it's turned off). This dish is also delicious with strawberries or peaches when they are in season.

FOR THE RASPBERRY SYRUP

¾ cup fresh raspberries

I tablespoon superfine sugar

FOR THE MERINGUE

9 egg whites, at room temperature

2½ cups superfine sugar

2 teaspoons cornstarch

I teaspoon white wine vinegar

I tablespoon rosewater

FOR THE FILLING

2 cups heavy whipping cream

I tablespoon confectioners' sugar

I tablespoon rosewater

1¼ cups fresh raspberries

Preheat the oven to 325°F and line a baking sheet with parchment paper.

First make the syrup: Combine the raspberries and sugar in a small saucepan, place over low heat, and stir until the sugar has completely dissolved. Cook for another 2–3 minutes until the raspberries have turned to mush. Transfer the raspberries to a sieve over a bowl and push them through the sieve using the back of a spoon to create a thick, syruplike consistency. Allow to cool.

To make the meringue, place the egg whites in a very clean and dry large bowl or the bowl of a stand mixer and use an electric hand mixer or the whisk attachment on the stand mixer to whisk until firm peaks form. Gradually add the superfine sugar, a tablespoon at a time, whisking constantly until the mixture is thick and glossy and the sugar has completely dissolved. Then add the cornstarch, vinegar, and rosewater and gently fold in until just combined.

Spoon the meringue onto the lined baking sheet to form a round and use the back of a wooden spoon to shape the meringue into a nest. Using a teaspoon, drizzle half the raspberry syrup around the meringue to create a ripple effect.

Place the meringue in the oven, reduce the oven temperature to 275°F, and bake for 1½ hours. Then turn off the oven, open the oven door, and leave the meringue to cool completely.

When the meringue has cooled and you are ready to serve, start assembling the filling—you don't want to add it too far in advance, as it will soak into the meringue. Gently whip the cream in a bowl until it thickens and then whisk in the confectioners' sugar. Fold in the rosewater. Spoon the filling into the center of the meringue, arrange the fresh raspberries on top, and drizzle with the remaining raspberry syrup.

Carrageen Moss Puddings with Carrageen Fritters

SERVES 4

Carrageen moss is a seaweed, but it's not strong in flavor, more a gentle taste of the sea as well as a fantastic natural setting agent. The texture of these puddings is fluffy and creamy. I use the leftover carrageen leaves for fritters—just dry them off, dip them in the batter, and fry, which you can do a day ahead. The best place to find carrageen moss is in health food stores or online—you only need a little, so a bag will go a long way. The pudding itself can also be made a day ahead and is simply delicious just served with a spoon of softly whipped cream and a sprinkle of brown sugar.

¼ ounce dried carrageen moss (Irish moss)

2 cups milk

2½ tablespoons superfine sugar

1 vanilla bean

1 egg, separated

FOR THE FRITTERS

½ cup buttermilk

1 egg

1 tablespoon superfine sugar, plus 3 tablespoons for coating

⅔ cup all-purpose flour

1 teaspoon baking powder

¾ cup vegetable oil

½ teaspoon ground cinnamon

Soak the carrageen moss in a bowl of lukewarm water for 15 minutes. Drain and place in a saucepan with the milk, 1 tablespoon of the sugar, and the vanilla bean. Bring to a boil, then reduce the heat and simmer for 30 minutes or until the mixture has thickened to the consistency of yogurt.

Transfer the mixture to a sieve set over a bowl and push the natural gelatin from the carrageen moss through the sieve with the back of a spoon. Don't discard the cooked carrageen moss, as you will be using it for the fritters, so rinse it under cold water and set aside.

Place the egg yolk in a bowl and whisk in the remaining 1½ tablespoons of sugar, then whisk in the strained milk mixture.

Place the egg white in a very clean and dry bowl and whisk until stiff, then fold into the milk mixture with a metal spoon. Divide the pudding mixture between four small bowls and chill in the fridge for about an hour or until set.

To make the carrageen moss fritters, add the buttermilk, egg, and tablespoon of sugar to a bowl and whisk together. In a separate bowl, mix the flour and baking powder together, then add to the buttermilk mixture and whisk together until smooth—the batter should be thick.

Place a frying pan over medium–high heat and pour in the vegetable oil. Once the oil is hot, dip the reserved pieces of carrageen moss into the batter and then straight into the hot oil. Fry until they are golden and crispy. Transfer to a bowl. Mix the remaining sugar and the cinnamon together, then toss the fritters in the cinnamon sugar.

Once the puddings have set, arrange the fritters on top and serve.

Orange Blossom Summer Cake with Cream & Strawberries

MAKES 1 CAKE

This is such a showstopping cake! I just love seeing everyone's faces as I bring it to the table. The orange blossom is so soft and delicate, and adds a beautiful subtle flavor of orange to the cake. You can make the cakes a day ahead and then assemble with the cream and fruit before you serve. This is gorgeous served as a dessert for a big supper or at an afternoon get-together.

6 eggs

1²/₃ cups superfine sugar

2²/₃ cups self-rising flour, sifted

2 teaspoons baking powder, sifted

3 sticks of unsalted butter, softened, plus extra for greasing

2 tablespoons orange blossom water

1 teaspoon vanilla extract

FOR THE FILLING

2 cups heavy whipping cream

1 tablespoon orange blossom water

²/₃ cup confectioners' sugar, sifted, plus extra for dusting

20-ounce jar strawberry jam

TO DECORATE

12 fresh strawberries

grated zest of 1 orange

Preheat the oven to 350°F. Grease three 8-inch sandwich cake pans and line the bottom of each pan with parchment paper.

Crack the eggs into a large bowl, then add the superfine sugar, flour, baking powder, butter, orange blossom water, and vanilla extract. Beat all the ingredients together with an electric hand mixer or a wooden spoon until well-combined.

Spoon the cake batter evenly between the prepared cake pans and tap the sides to release any air bubbles. Bake for 25 minutes or until the cakes are lightly golden brown.

Remove the cakes from the oven, let cool in the pans for about 15 minutes, then remove from the pans and transfer to a wire rack to cool completely.

While the cakes are cooling, prepare the filling: Lightly whip the cream, orange blossom water, and confectioners' sugar together in a bowl until light and fluffy.

To assemble, place one of the cakes, top facing downward, on a cake plate or stand. Spread with some of the strawberry jam, followed by half the cream mixture. Repeat the process with another sponge, then add the third sponge, top facing upwards. Arrange the strawberries on top, then dust with confectioners' sugar and sprinkle with the orange zest.

Sweet Geranium Cheesecake

MAKES 1 CHEESECAKE

The sweet geranium lends a beautifully delicate honey and lemon flavor to this cheesecake and the flowers look so pretty on top! I always have sweet geranium plants growing because they are great for using in baking, infusing creams, and in syrups. If you don't have any sweet geranium leaves, you can use lemon verbena instead.

5 tablespoons butter, plus extra for greasing

5½ ounces ginger snaps (about 2 cups)

5½ ounces graham crackers (about 10 sheets)

8 sweet geranium leaves, plus 10 for decoration, thoroughly washed

1¼ cups heavy cream

1½ cups cream cheese

¾ cup superfine sugar

First make the cheesecake crust: Lightly grease an 8-inch springform cake pan or tart pan. Melt the butter in a small saucepan over medium heat. Add the ginger snaps and graham crackers to a food processor and process to crumbs. Transfer to a bowl, pour the melted butter over the crumbs, and mix together well. Transfer the buttery crumbs to the greased pan, using the back of a spoon to spread and press them into an even, well-compacted base. Chill in the fridge for at least 30 minutes until firm and cold.

Add the eight sweet geranium leaves to a saucepan and stir in the cream. Place over low heat, bring to a simmer, and continue simmering for 10 minutes. Remove the pan from the heat and leave the cream to cool completely and infuse—about an hour.

Remove the geranium leaves from the cooled cream and then whip the cream.

Beat the cream cheese and sugar together in a large bowl until the sugar has dissolved and the mixture is smooth, then fold in the sweet geranium-infused whipped cream.

Spread the cheesecake mixture on top of the crust and arrange the extra sweet geranium leaves (or any decorative flowers) on top. Chill in the fridge for 2–3 hours until set before serving.

Berry Trifle

SERVES 8

This trifle sings of summer—delicious pops of sweet summer berries, creamy mascarpone whipped with custard and infused with vanilla and set on Madeira or pound cake. On the 4th of July, I top this trifle with flaming sparklers or mini American flags—it's my American hero dessert! You can make it up to a day ahead and it's great for entertaining a crowd. You can also serve it in smaller individual bowls, but try to use glass so that you see the fabulous colors and layers.

3 cups fresh blueberries

3 cups fresh raspberries

$1/3$ cup superfine sugar

3 tablespoons crème de cassis (optional)

10½-ounce Madeira cake, sliced

2 cups cold custard

1¾ cups mascarpone cheese

1 tablespoon vanilla extract

1¼ cups heavy cream, softly whipped

Place two-thirds of both berries and all the sugar in a saucepan and simmer over low heat for 2 minutes. Pour in the crème de cassis, if using, then remove the pan from the heat and let the mixture cool.

Arrange a layer of the madeira cake slices in the bottom of a large trifle bowl, then spoon the berry mixture on top.

Add the custard, mascarpone, and vanilla extract to a large bowl and whisk together until smooth, but ensure that the mixture doesn't become runny, as you want it to remain slightly thick. Spoon on top of the berry mixture, followed by the softly whipped cream.

Cover the bowl with plastic wrap and chill in the fridge for a couple of hours. Just before serving, decorate the top of the trifle with the remaining berries.

Barbecued Peaches with Rosemary & Maple Butter

SERVES 6

The first time I had this dish was about ten years ago at a wedding in Tuscany, when they were served as the dessert. A grill was set up under a line of olive trees, and the juicy peaches were perfectly grilled, then passed along for a drizzle of rosemary maple butter and a dollop of mascarpone. They were sensational! I add a crumble of amaretti cookie on top as it brings great texture.

6 ripe peaches

woody rosemary stalks, for skewers (or use wooden skewers)

16 tablespoons (2 sticks) butter

2 tablespoons chopped rosemary leaves

2 tablespoons maple syrup

$^2/_3$ cup mascarpone

6 amaretti cookies, crumbled

Slice the ripe peaches in half through the middle and remove the pits. Thread the peach halves onto the rosemary stalks or wooden skewers.

Prepare a charcoal grill or heat a gas grill to high heat, or place a grill pan over high heat. Grill the peaches, turning the skewers frequently, for about 10 minutes until they are soft.

While the peaches are grilling, place a saucepan over low heat and add the butter, rosemary, and maple syrup. Stir until the butter has melted, then let simmer for 5 minutes. Remove the pan from the heat.

Transfer the grilled peaches to dessert plates and drizzle the hot rosemary and maple butter over the peaches, followed by a dollop of mascarpone and a sprinkle of crumbled amaretti cookies to serve.

Fall Suppers

Menus

FALL GATHERING

BROILED MUSSELS WITH CHORIZO
& FLAT-LEAF PARSLEY BREAD CRUMBS

SALMON FISH CAKES WITH
HORSERADISH CREAM

BANANA CAKE WITH
COCONUT FROSTING

FARMHOUSE CHEESE SUPPER

IRISH FARMHOUSE CHEESE SOUFFLÉ

COOLEA CHEESE POTATO DUMPLINGS
WITH SAGE BUTTER

ROASTED HAZELNUT
HOT CHOCOLATE PUDDINGS

FIRESIDE SUPPER

SALMON RILLETTES

CREAMY PARMESAN POLENTA
WITH BLOOD SAUSAGE

STICKY FIGGY CAKE

NEW YORK HARVEST

SMOKED HADDOCK & CORN CHOWDER

ROAST BUTTERNUT SQUASH, BLUE
CHEESE & SAFFRON PAPPARDELLE

BAKED APPLES WITH DATES & SPICES
SERVED WITH VANILLA CUSTARD

NORTHERN ITALIAN WILD
MUSHROOM SUPPER

WILD MUSHROOMS, LEMON & THYME
WITH RUNNY POACHED EGG

ROAST TARRAGON CHICKEN WITH
MUSHROOM RISOTTO

VANILLA PANNA COTTA
WITH HONEYED FIGS

ONE-POT FALL SUPPER

HONEY & THYME-ROASTED FIGS, RICOTTA
& SOURDOUGH TOAST

CHOCOLATE BEEF CHILI WITH
JALAPEÑO & CHEESE SCONES

ORANGE, PISTACHIO & YOGURT CAKE

SUNDAY ROAST

SPICED BUTTERNUT SQUASH &
COCONUT SOUP WITH PUMPKIN
SEED BREAD

ROAST PORK WITH APPLES
& BLACKBERRIES

BLACKBERRY BUTTER CRUST PIE

Honey & Thyme-Roasted Figs, Ricotta & Sourdough Toast

SERVES 6

Where I live in London, I have the most fantastic tropical garden with an enormous fig tree, and during fall I have an endless supply of delicious, ripe figs. These figs simply roasted with thyme and honey are heavenly. You could leave out the sourdough toast if you wish and serve it as is.

12 fresh ripe figs

3 tablespoons Irish (or locally sourced) honey

2 tablespoons olive oil

1 tablespoon chopped thyme leaves

sea salt and freshly ground black pepper

6 slices of sourdough bread

12 ounces ricotta cheese

1 cup walnuts, chopped

Preheat the oven to 350°F.

Cut the figs into quarters and place on a baking sheet.

Mix the honey, olive oil, and thyme together in a small bowl. Drizzle half the mixture over the figs and toss to coat, or use a pastry brush to paint the figs with the mixture. Season with salt and pepper. Roast for 10 minutes.

While the figs are roasting, toast the sourdough bread, then cut the slices in half.

Arrange the sourdough toast, ricotta, walnuts, and the roasted figs on a sharing platter or individual plates and drizzle the remaining honey mixture over the figs and ricotta.

To eat, spread the ricotta onto the sourdough toast, followed by the honey and thyme figs, and add a sprinkle of chopped walnuts on top.

Wild Mushrooms, Lemon & Thyme with Runny Poached Egg

SERVES 2

This dish reminds me so much of the falls when I lived in Italy. When the wild mushrooms were in season, the market in the square in Turin would be filled with farmers selling amazing varieties from the Langhe region nearby. The soft-boiled egg oozing over the earthy mushrooms is utterly delicious! If you don't want to add the egg, then use shavings of Parmesan cheese instead.

7 ounces wild mushrooms, such as chanterelles or morels

2 tablespoons butter

2 tablespoons extra virgin olive oil

1 garlic clove, crushed

sea salt and freshly ground black pepper

juice of 1 lemon

1 tablespoon finely chopped thyme leaves

2 eggs

sourdough bread, to serve

Clean any grit off the mushrooms using a soft brush, then chop them up coarsely.

Place a large frying pan over medium heat and add the butter and olive oil. Once the butter has melted, toss in the mushrooms and crushed garlic, season with salt and pepper, and add the lemon juice. Increase the heat and cook, tossing, for 3 minutes.

Sprinkle the thyme over the mushrooms and cook for another minute.

While the mushrooms are cooking, poach the eggs in a saucepan of salted boiling water for just 4 minutes, then remove with a slotted spoon and drain on paper towels.

Divide the cooked mushrooms between two warmed plates and place a runny poached egg in the center of each serving. Serve with fresh sourdough bread.

Irish Farmhouse Cheese Soufflé

MAKES 6 INDIVIDUAL SOUFFLÉS

These are my beautiful, light, fluffy cheese clouds! They make a dreamy appetizer or lunch. If you are frightened of the thought of making a soufflé, please don't be, as this recipe is so simple and completely foolproof. I also love making this with Gouda or Gruyère. It's best to make the mixture no more than 2 hours before cooking, as you might lose the lightness in the egg white.

3 tablespoons fresh white bread crumbs

3 tablespoons butter, plus extra for greasing

1/3 cup all-purpose flour

1 1/4 cups milk

1 1/2 cups mature Irish Cheddar, grated

1 teaspoon Dijon mustard

4 large eggs, separated

Preheat the oven to 400°F. Grease six small ramekins or other small ovenproof dishes and sprinkle with the bread crumbs to coat.

Melt the butter in a saucepan over medium heat. Stir in the flour and cook, continuing to stir, until a paste (roux) forms. Gradually add the milk, whisking constantly, and cook until you have a smooth, thickened sauce.

Whisk in the grated Cheddar and mustard, followed by the egg yolks. Once the cheese has melted into the sauce and the consistency is smooth, remove the pan from the heat.

Put a pot of water on to boil. Whisk the egg whites in a very clean and dry bowl until stiff. Stir a couple of spoonfuls into the cheese mixture to loosen it, then very slowly and gently fold in the remaining egg whites with a spatula. Divide the mixture between the prepared dishes.

Make a bain-marie by half-filling a roasting pan with the boiling water and place in the oven. Stand the dishes in the bain-marie and bake for 12 minutes until the soufflés are well-risen and golden, then serve immediately.

Smoked Haddock & Corn Chowder

SERVES 6

Where I was born in Cork, Ireland, is also home to some of the world's best fish smokers, which means that I grew up eating lots of smoked fish. This smoked haddock chowder is one of my favorite ways to cook with it. The delicious smoky flavors infuse the creamy soup and the sweetness of the corn during the fall adds a ray of sunshine and sweetness. Make it in big batches so you can freeze ahead.

3 tablespoons butter

1 large potato, peeled and diced

1 onion, finely diced

1 leek, finely sliced

2 celery ribs, finely sliced

2 garlic cloves, crushed

½ cup dry white wine

2 cups hot fish stock

1¼ cups milk

1 corn on the cob, husk and silky threads removed

2¼ pounds smoked haddock fillet, skin removed and cut into small chunks

1 cup half-and-half

2 tablespoons chopped dill

sea salt and freshly ground black pepper

Place a saucepan over medium heat and add the butter. Once the butter has melted, add the potatoes, onion, leek, celery, and garlic, stir well, and cover the pan with a lid. Reduce the heat to low and leave the vegetables to sweat for 5 minutes, stirring once or twice.

Remove the pan from the heat and stir in the white wine. Return the pan to medium heat and cook, uncovered, for 3–4 minutes.

Pour in the stock and milk and bring to a boil, then reduce the heat and simmer for 10 minutes.

Stand the corn cob upright on its base and run a sharp knife down its sides all around to remove the kernels, then add them to the saucepan. Gently stir in the haddock and simmer for 5 minutes.

Stir in the half-and-half and dill and season to taste with salt and pepper. Cook for another 5 minutes, then serve in warmed bowls alongside my Rosemary Clodagh Bread (page 203), if you wish.

Broiled Mussels with Chorizo
& Flat-leaf Parsley Bread Crumbs

SERVES 6

Plump, sweet mussels with spicy, juicy chorizo, peppery flat-leaf parsley, aromatic garlic, and crispy buttered bread crumbs—sounds delicious, right? And it's so incredibly easy to make. This is the perfect easy appetizer to serve for supper or as a main course at lunch. You can get the mussels prepared a day ahead and then just pop them under the broiler before you serve. You can leave the chorizo out if you want a simpler garlic and herb flavor.

2¼ pounds live mussels, cleaned and beards removed (see page 85)

½ cup water

3 tablespoons butter, softened

3 garlic cloves, crushed

2 ounces cooking chorizo, skin removed and diced

2 tablespoons chopped flat-leaf parsley

½ cup fresh white bread crumbs

sea salt and freshly ground black pepper

Place the mussels in a saucepan with the water and bring to a boil over high heat. Cover the pan with a lid and steam for 3 minutes or until all the mussels have opened (discard any that remain closed).

Drain the mussels, and when cool enough to handle, pull away and discard the top shells, leaving the mussels in the bottom shells. Place the mussels on a baking sheet.

Preheat the broiler to high. Add all the remaining ingredients to a bowl and season with salt and pepper, then mix well, using the back of a spoon to blend them together.

Spoon the bread crumb mixture over the mussels using a teaspoon and flatten gently. Cook under the hot broiler for 2–3 minutes until well-browned. Serve.

Salmon Rillettes

SERVES 4

I love serving these salmon rillettes as a sharing platter on a serving board with thinly sliced sourdough toast and pickles. You can get it made a couple of days before serving and it also works really well as picnic food or a packed lunch.

1¾ cups dry white wine

2 shallots, finely chopped

14 ounces skinless salmon fillet, chopped

3½ ounces smoked salmon, chopped

⅔ cup crème fraîche

2 teaspoons finely chopped capers

1 tablespoon finely chopped dill

grated zest and juice of 1 lemon

sea salt and freshly ground black pepper

TO SERVE

thinly sliced sourdough bread, toasted

pickles

Place the white wine and shallots in a saucepan over medium heat and bring to a boil, then reduce the heat to low. Add the fresh salmon and poach for 5 minutes. Using a slotted spoon, transfer the salmon to a plate lined with paper towels to drain. Strain the poaching liquid through a sieve, discarding the liquid, and transfer the shallots to a bowl. Add the poached salmon, cover the bowl with plastic wrap, and chill in the fridge until completely cooled.

Add the remaining ingredients to the poached salmon, season with salt and pepper, and gently mix just to combine—the poached salmon will break up a little, but don't overmix or the mixture will turn to a paste. Cover the bowl again and chill in the fridge.

Serve the salmon rillettes with thinly sliced, toasted sourdough bread and some pickles.

Spiced Butternut Squash & Coconut Soup with Pumpkin Seed Bread

SERVES 6

FOR THE PUMPKIN SEED BREAD

1½ cups all-purpose flour, plus extra for dusting

1 teaspoon baking soda

1 teaspoon fine sea salt

2¾ cups whole wheat flour

2 tablespoons pumpkin seeds

1½ cups milk, plus extra for brushing

1 cup plain yogurt, plus extra for brushing

FOR THE SOUP

1 tablespoon butter

2¼ pounds butternut squash, peeled, seeded, and cut into 1-inch pieces

1 teaspoon ground cumin

1 teaspoon garam masala

2 garlic cloves, crushed

1¼ cups onions, chopped

3 cups hot vegetable stock

1¼ cups coconut milk

sea salt and freshly ground black pepper

TO GARNISH

pumpkin seeds

raw coconut flakes

This soup is a ray of sunshine in a bowl during grayer days in the fall. The butternut squash is so sweet and creamy in the soup, and I love spicing and warming it up with cumin and garam masala. It does make a huge difference if you make your own vegetable stock.

Preheat the oven to 425°F. Dust a baking sheet with all-purpose flour.

To make the bread, sift the all-purpose flour, baking soda, and salt into a large bowl, then add the whole wheat flour. Using clean hands, mix the dry ingredients together with half the pumpkin seeds, then make a well in the center.

Whisk the milk and yogurt together in a bowl, then slowly pour into the well and use your free hand to mix the dry mixture into the wet mixture, trying to spread your fingers far apart so that your hand resembles a trough. Ensure that the resulting dough is entirely wet, with no dry patches remaining.

Pat your hands with all-purpose flour and shape the dough into a round. Place on the floured baking sheet. Dust a large knife with all-purpose flour and use to cut the shape of a cross into the top of the dough, cutting about two-thirds of the way down through the dough.

Using a pastry brush, brush the dough with extra milk and yogurt mixed together. Sprinkle the remaining pumpkin seeds on top and press them gently into the dough. Bake for 25 minutes, then reduce the oven to 350°F, and bake for another 20 minutes. To test whether the loaf is cooked, tap the bottom—it should sound hollow. Transfer to a wire rack to cool.

To make the soup, place a heavy-bottomed saucepan over medium heat and melt the butter. Add the squash, spices, garlic, and onions, and season with salt and pepper. Stir well, then reduce the heat to low, cover the pan with a lid, and sweat for about 15 minutes, stirring every 5 minutes or so.

Stir in the hot stock and coconut milk and bring to a boil, then let cook, uncovered, for about 15 minutes until the squash is tender. Transfer the soup to a blender or food processor and blend to a smooth consistency.

Return the soup to the saucepan and reheat. Serve in warmed bowls, topped with pumpkin seeds and coconut flakes, along with the pumpkin seed bread.

ROUND/DURING THE TIME OF YOUR MENSES. I LIKE TO STEEP AT LEAST
¼TH CUP – ½ CUP HERBS IN A 32oz MASON JAR (HOT WATER) OVERNIGHT.
IN THE MORNING, I STRAIN THE HERBS, GIVE THEM A GOOD SQUEEZE, & STEEP
IN WATER AGAIN. I DRINK THE FIRST ROUND THROUGHOUT THE DAY & SECOND
ROUND WHEN IM HOME FROM WORK. SOME FOLKS EXPERIENCE EXTREME PAIN.
I CANT GUARANTEE IT'LL TAKE ALL THE PAIN AWAY BUT IT SHOULD HELP.

CELEBRATORY ~ A JUICY, TART BLEND TO HELP IMPROVE MOOD & CIRCULATION!
GREAT ALONE, EVEN BETTER IN COCKTAILS/MOCKTAILS. STEEP, ADD HONEY, LET
CHILL, THEN MIX WITH FRESH SQUEEZED CITRUS JUICE & TOP WITH SPARKLING
WATER/KOMBUCHA. PAIRS WELL WITH TEQUILA, VODKA, & GIN. I HIGHLY
ENCOURAGE YOU TO GET CREATIVE WITH THIS BLEND! PAIRS REALLY WELL WITH
THE SPIRIT SONG APHRODISIAC TINCTURE FOR AN EXTRA FESTIVE KICK!

BREATHE EASY ~ WINTER WELLNESS IS IMPORTANT! WINTER IS COLD & DRY,
THIS BLEND KEEPS YOUR MUCUS MEMBRANES HYDRATED, MAKING IT EASIER
FOR YOUR BODY TO FLUSH OUT TOXINS. WARMING HERBS SYNERGIZE THE BLEND!

HOPE THESE ITEMS AID YOU ON YOUR JOURNEY, HELP YOU FEEL YOUR
BEST, & BRING JOY TO YOUR LIFE. LET ME KNOW IF ANY QUESTIONS COME UP.
TAKE CARE UNTIL NEXT TIME!

❀ *enjoy!* ❀

— NATALIE
SUN GLOW BOTANICALS
IG: SUNGLOW.BOTANICALS

DARCI! ♥

MANY THANK YOUS TO YOU FOR CHOOSING TO SUPPORT MY
SMALL BUSINESS & TRYING OUT MY OFFERINGS. I HOPE 2021
HAS BEEN TREATING YOU WELL, I HOPE YOU'VE BEEN SHEDDING
THE LAYERS/THINGS/HABITS THAT NO LONGER SERVE YOU IN
ORDER TO MAKE ROOM FOR NEW GROWTH.

GENTLE ~ A WONDERFUL COMPANION WHENEVER YOU NEED
TENDERNESS IN YOUR LIFE. ENJOY ALONE OR FOR AN EXTRA
SPECIAL TREAT, ADD HONEY & NUT MILK/MILK FOR GENTLE
MILK TEA! GREAT AS A FACE STEAM OR BATH/FOOT SOAK.
ENJOY OFTEN, TAKE DEEP BREATHES, LET THE STRESSES &
TENSION SLOWLY MELT AWAY.

MOON MAGIC ~ A VERY NUTRIENT DENSE BLEND TO HELP
ENERGIZE YOU, CLEAR STAGNATION, & HELP YOU FEEL BETTER

→

Roast Pork with Apples & Blackberries

SERVES 6

1½ cups apples, peeled, cored, and diced

30 fresh blackberries

1 onion, finely diced

1 tablespoon finely chopped rosemary leaves

⅓ cup fresh white bread crumbs

3 tablespoons butter, melted

sea salt and freshly ground black pepper

3¼ pounds boneless pork loin

3 rosemary sprigs

FOR THE APPLE CHIPS

2 crisp apples

ground cinnamon, for dusting

FOR THE APPLE & BLACKBERRY SAUCE

3 cups apples, peeled, cored, and coarsely chopped

20 fresh blackberries

2 tablespoons superfine sugar

3 tablespoons butter

½ cup water

1 rosemary sprig

Every fall, I go blackberry picking in the country. It's something I start to look forward to at the end of summer, and taking an afternoon to walk along the country roads with a basket in hand foraging for the plumpest berries is heaven. Their juicy sweetness with the sour cooking apples, soaking into the pork while it roasts, is incredible. The apple chips are so simple to make and look fabulous dotted around the serving dish. I like to serve a creamy gratin dauphinoise with this dish or simple buttery mashed potatoes.

Preheat the oven to 425°F.

Add the apples, blackberries, onion, chopped rosemary, bread crumbs, and melted butter to a large bowl, season with salt and pepper, and mix well.

Butterfly the pork loin by making a slit down its length, cutting just deep enough so that you can open the loin up to lie flat like a book; don't cut all the way through.

Spoon the stuffing mixture onto the meat and spread it evenly, then close up the meat and secure it in its original shape by tying it together at intervals with kitchen string, tucking the rosemary sprigs under the string. Push in any stuffing that escapes from the ends.

Rub the pork all over with salt and pepper and place in a roasting pan. Roast for 25 minutes, then reduce the oven temperature to 350°F and roast for another 1 hour 10 minutes (or 20 minutes per pound).

While the pork is roasting, prepare the apple chips: Core the apples and slice very thinly through the middle. Dust with cinnamon and lay on a baking sheet lined with parchment paper.

Bake in the oven with the pork (at the lower temperature) for 45 minutes– 1 hour, turning halfway through, until dried out and light golden, checking and removing any chips that are ready as and when.

Meanwhile, make the apple and blackberry sauce: Place all the ingredients in a saucepan, cover the pan with a lid, and cook gently, stirring every so often, for 15–20 minutes until the apples start to break down.

Once the pork is cooked, pour about ½ cup of the cooking juices into the sauce and stir well.

Serve slices of pork with the hot apple and blackberry sauce and apple chips.

3 tablespoons salted butter

10½ ounces ground beef

1 small white onion or shallot, finely chopped

1-inch piece of fresh ginger, peeled and grated

3 garlic cloves, crushed

1 teaspoon ground cumin

1 teaspoon ground cinnamon

3 small dried chiles, chopped

3½ ounces smoked thick-cut bacon, chopped

3½ ounces fully cured, ready-to-eat chorizo, diced

⅔ cup red wine

14-ounce can cherry tomatoes

1¼ cups water

1 tablespoon brown sugar

2 teaspoons finely chopped fresh or dried oregano

2 bay leaves

1 tablespoon ketchup

sea salt and freshly ground black pepper

2 ounces dark chocolate, grated

14-ounce can red kidney beans, rinsed and drained

FOR THE JALAPEÑO & CHEESE SCONES

1¾ cups all-purpose flour, plus extra for dusting

1 tablespoon baking powder

pinch of fine sea salt

3 tablespoons salted butter, chilled and cubed

1 cup Dubliner cheese, grated

2 fresh jalapeño chiles, finely chopped

½–⅔ cup milk or buttermilk

Chocolate Beef Chili with Jalapeño & Cheese Scones

SERVES 6

The chocolate in this utterly delicious chili adds a fantastic silky texture as well as deep notes of cocoa. I always double the recipe when I am making it and freeze half. It's always better made the day ahead as the flavors improve over time.

Place a Dutch oven or heavy pot over medium heat and add half the butter. Once the butter has melted, add the ground beef and cook, stirring and breaking up with a wooden spoon, until browned. Transfer to a plate.

Add the remaining butter to the pot and stir in the onion or shallot, ginger, and garlic. Cook for 2 minutes, then stir in the cumin, cinnamon, and dried chiles. Cook for another minute. Add the chopped bacon and chorizo and cook, stirring, for about 3 minutes until lovely and crispy.

Return the beef to the pan and stir well. Pour in the red wine, stir, and cook for 2 minutes. Then add the cherry tomatoes, water, brown sugar, oregano, bay leaves, and ketchup, season with salt and pepper, and stir well. Cover the pan with a lid and simmer over low heat for 2 hours.

While the chilli is cooking, make the scones: Preheat the oven to 400°F and dust a baking sheet with flour.

Sift the flour, baking powder, and salt into a large bowl. Add the butter and rub in with your fingertips until the mixture resembles fine bread crumbs.

Stir in half the grated cheese, followed by half the jalapeño chiles. Then gradually mix in enough milk or buttermilk with a fork to make a soft dough.

Roll out the dough on a floured work surface into a round about ½-inch thick. Cut into six wedges, place on the floured baking sheet, and sprinkle the remaining cheese and jalapeños on top. Bake for 15 minutes until golden brown. Transfer the scones to a wire rack and let cool for 10 minutes.

Remove the lid of the pot and stir in the dark chocolate and kidney beans, then simmer, uncovered, for another 15 minutes. Serve with the jalapeño and cheese scones.

Salmon Fish Cakes with Horseradish Cream

SERVES 4

I make these fish cakes when I am having a relaxed supper at home. They are so simple to cook—just combine all the ingredients together and shape into patties. You can make them a day ahead, and they also freeze very well. Fresh horseradish cream is a delicious peppery combo with the salmon, and I also love serving the fish cakes with a chile and tomato salsa or with a smoked paprika aioli (page 192).

FOR THE SALMON FISH CAKES

14 ounces Russet potatoes, boiled and mashed

14 ounces skinless salmon fillet, poached and flaked

2 scallions, finely chopped

2 teaspoons capers

1 tablespoon finely chopped dill

grated zest and juice of ½ lemon

3 tablespoons butter

sea salt and freshly ground black pepper

FOR THE FRESH HORSERADISH CREAM

½ cup crème fraîche

1 tablespoon peeled and grated fresh horseradish root

grated zest and juice of ½ lemon

2 teaspoons finely chopped flat-leaf parsley

1 lemon, cut into wedges, plus a bunch of watercress (optional), to serve

Preheat the oven to 350°F.

Place all the ingredients for the fish cakes except the butter in a large bowl and season with salt and pepper. Mix until all the ingredients are well-combined. Divide the fish cake mixture into four balls and shape each into a patty.

Place a frying pan over medium heat and add the butter. Once the butter has melted, add the fish cakes and brown on both sides. Transfer the fish cakes to a baking sheet and bake for 10 minutes.

While the fish cakes are baking, mix all the ingredients for the horseradish cream together in a small bowl and season with salt and pepper.

To serve, place each fish cake on a warmed plate with a spoonful of the horseradish cream and a wedge of lemon, plus a handful of watercress, if you wish.

Roast Tarragon Chicken with Mushroom Risotto

SERVES 4

This is my favorite way to cook and serve roast chicken during the fall. The tarragon adds a delicious sweet flavor, mixed with the spicy Dijon mustard and aromatic garlic. The risotto is creamy, so there is no need for a sauce. It's an ideal supper for a cozy evening at home.

7 tablespoons butter, softened

2 garlic cloves, crushed

3 tablespoons finely chopped tarragon

2 teaspoons Dijon mustard

sea salt and freshly ground black pepper

1 whole organic or free-range chicken, about 3 pounds

FOR THE MUSHROOM RISOTTO

7 tablespoons butter

2 shallots, very finely chopped

2 garlic cloves, crushed

1½ cups Arborio (risotto) rice

½ cup dry white wine

3 cups hot chicken or vegetable stock

9 ounces button mushrooms, sliced

1 tablespoon finely chopped thyme leaves, plus extra to garnish

¾ cup Parmesan cheese, grated

1 tablespoon mascarpone cheese

Preheat the oven to 400°F.

Start by prepping the chicken: Add the softened butter, garlic, tarragon, and mustard to a bowl, season with salt and pepper, and mix well, using the back of a spoon to blend the ingredients together. Using clean hands, smear the butter mixture all over the chicken as well as underneath the skin.

Place the chicken in a roasting pan and roast for 1½ hours or until cooked through. To check if the chicken is cooked, insert a skewer into the thickest part of the thigh—the juices should run clear.

Meanwhile, to make the risotto, place a large saucepan over medium heat and add half the butter. Once the butter has melted, stir in the shallots and garlic, then cover the pan with a lid, reduce the heat to low, and leave to sweat for about 2 minutes until the shallots are softened but not browned.

Add the rice and stir to coat it with the butter, then cook, stirring, for a couple of minutes. Season with salt and pepper. Pour in the white wine, stir, and cook for about 2 minutes until almost all of it has been absorbed.

Add the hot stock a ladleful at a time, cooking while stirring constantly after adding the stock until it has been absorbed before adding more. It should take 15–20 minutes for the rice to be cooked, but check by tasting as you go.

While the risotto is cooking, place a frying pan over high heat, add the remaining butter and the mushrooms, and cook, tossing, for 3 minutes. About 5 minutes before the rice is cooked, stir in the mushrooms and thyme, then stir in the Parmesan and mascarpone just before you serve the risotto.

Once the chicken is cooked, transfer it to a large serving platter and spoon the risotto all around it, then garnish with extra thyme.

Coolea Cheese Potato Dumplings with Sage Butter

SERVES 4

Potato dumplings are a fantastic way to use up leftover mashed potatoes. You can also make these with sweet potatoes or add different cheeses to the mix. The dumplings have great texture—soft on the inside like little pillows and crispy on the outside. The sage butter is something I learned when living in Italy and is so delicious with these cheese dumplings or with egg tagliolini.

FOR THE POTATO DUMPLINGS

2¼ pounds Russet potatoes, unpeeled and washed

2½ cups all-purpose flour, plus extra for dusting

9 ounces Coolea cheese, or use a mature Gruyère cheese, grated (about 2 cups)

1 egg yolk

sea salt and freshly ground black pepper

FOR THE SAGE BUTTER

7 tablespoons salted butter

2 tablespoons finely chopped sage

For the potato dumplings, place the whole potatoes in a large saucepan, with the largest ones at the bottom, and fill the pan halfway with water. Cover the pan with a lid and place over high heat. When the water begins to boil, drain off about half so that there is just enough left in the pan for the potatoes to steam. Allow to steam, covered, for 30–40 minutes, depending on the size of the potatoes, until soft.

Once the potatoes are cooked, hold them in a kitchen towel while you peel them. Place them in a bowl and mash well or put through a potato ricer.

Mix the flour, grated cheese, and egg yolk into the potatoes, and season with 2 teaspoons of salt and some pepper. Transfer the dough to a lightly floured work surface and knead lightly until well-combined. Shape into three or four balls.

Dust the surface with more flour if necessary. Using your fingertips, roll each ball of dough into a sausage about ¾-inch in diameter. Cut into 1-inch pieces, then roll each piece against the front tines of a fork to create ridges—this will help the sage butter cling to the dumplings once they are cooked.

Bring a large saucepan of salted water to a boil. Add the potato dumplings to the boiling water. When they rise to the surface, they are cooked, so quickly remove with a slotted spoon and drain well.

For the sage butter, place a frying pan over medium heat and add the butter. Once the butter has melted, add the sage and cook until it is slightly crispy.

Add the potato dumplings to the pan and mix them gently with the sage butter. Transfer to warmed serving plates and serve.

Roast Butternut Squash, Blue Cheese & Saffron Pappardelle

SERVES 2

This recipe is such a fast and easy dish to create and a great way to use up any leftover roasted butternut squash. I crumble in Cashel Blue cheese, my favorite from Tipperary in Ireland, which is creamy and chalky in texture and has that unique ashy/smoky flavor. (You can substitute other blue cheese if this is unavailable.) Next, a little crème fraîche to loosen it up and then comes the sunshine, as threads of saffron share their smokiness and enchanting color with the sauce. The fresh pasta goes for a hot boiling sea salt swim for two minutes, then straight into the sunshine sauce, so that the pasta absorbs the flavors like bread soaking up gravy. Toss in the sweet butternut squash and sprinkle crunchy pumpkin seeds on top, then open a bottle of Barbera d'Asti, which has a lovely soft texture, with blackberry and Morello cherry flavors, and goes perfectly with this pasta. And ahh, we are in Rome with love from my London kitchen.

1¼ pounds butternut squash

2 tablespoons olive oil

¾ cup crème fraîche

¾ cup Cashel Blue cheese (or other blue cheese)

½ teaspoon saffron threads

sea salt and freshly ground black pepper

9 ounces fresh pappardelle

3 tablespoons pumpkin seeds

Preheat the oven to 350°F.

Halve the butternut squash and peel away the outer skin (use a good-quality vegetable peeler to make the task easier). Slice the squash into quarters and scoop out and discard the seeds, then cut the flesh into ½-inch cubes.

Spread the squash out on a roasting pan, drizzle with the olive oil, and season with salt and pepper. Roast for 35 minutes (you will notice the squash turning wrinkly), stirring every 10 minutes to ensure that it is well-coated with the oil.

While the squash finishes roasting, place a frying pan over low heat, add the crème fraîche and cheese, and whisk together. Then whisk in the saffron and season with salt and pepper. Cook for another 3 minutes until the sauce begins to thicken.

Bring a large saucepan of salted water to a boil over high heat. Stir the pasta into the boiling water and cook for 3 minutes only—be careful, as it can very easily overcook.

Drain the pasta and return to the saucepan. Stir in the blue cheese and saffron sauce and the roasted squash and toss together really well, then transfer to a warmed serving dish. Sprinkle the pumpkin seeds on top before serving.

Creamy Parmesan Polenta with Blood Sausage

SERVES 4

I used to make creamy polenta like this when I lived in Turin in Northern Italy because the winters were so cold and this is such an easy and warming dish. The blood sausage adds great texture and flavors of sweetness as well as earthy spices. You will probably have some polenta left over, and if so, pour it into a dish, let it cool before you put it in the fridge where it will set, and you can then do a couple of things with it. You can slice it through the middle, add some fontina cheese, and bake it in the oven, or you can slice it thinly and then fry. It's also delicious served with roasted purple sprouting broccoli with Romesco sauce and crunchy seeds (see page 44).

²/₃ cup whole milk

2½ cups water

½ teaspoon sea salt

1 cup coarse polenta

1 tablespoon olive oil

10 ounces blood sausage

3 tablespoons butter

1 cup Parmesan cheese, grated

1 teaspoon dried oregano

Pour the milk into a large saucepan along with the water and salt and bring to a boil.

Once the liquid has come to a boil, pour in the polenta in a thin, steady stream, whisking constantly. Cook, stirring, for 1–2 minutes, until it thickens. Reduce the heat to low and cook, stirring well, about every 5 minutes to prevent it from sticking, for about 35–45 minutes until the polenta begins to come away from the sides of the pan.

While the polenta finishes cooking, place a frying pan over medium heat and add the olive oil. Cut the blood sausage into small pieces, add to the pan, and cook until it becomes nice and crispy on the outside, stirring every couple of minutes so that it cooks evenly.

Once the polenta is ready, add the butter, Parmesan, and oregano and stir until the butter and cheese have melted into the polenta.

Lastly, stir in the blood sausage and then serve.

Baked Apples with Dates & Spices served with Vanilla Custard

SERVES 4

My dad used to love making spiced baked apples for us when we were growing up. They are so simple to prep, and look equally fabulous on the plate. The dates, cinnamon, and nutmeg add delicious sweetness and spice to the apple, and there is nothing better to serve them with than a creamy custard. I do love to make my own custard, but if you are pressed for time, there are plenty of good store-bought versions that you can buy at the supermarket. Get the apples prepped a day ahead and then all that's left is to pop them in the oven before you sit down for the main course.

4 sweet apples

16 cloves

2 tablespoons Irish (or locally sourced) honey

4 dried pitted dates, finely chopped

2 teaspoons ground cinnamon

1 teaspoon freshly grated nutmeg

5 tablespoons butter, melted

FOR THE CUSTARD

1¾ cups milk

1 vanilla bean

3 egg yolks

2 tablespoons superfine sugar

1 teaspoon cornstarch

Preheat the oven to 350°F.

Remove the cores of the apples with an apple corer, then use a spoon to scoop out more of the apple to double the size of each cavity.

Stud around the middle of each apple with four cloves, then stand the apples in a shallow baking dish.

Place the honey, dates, cinnamon, nutmeg, and melted butter in a small bowl and whisk together, then pour the thick liquid into the cavity of each apple. Bake the apples for 30 minutes.

While the apples are baking, make the custard: Pour the milk into a saucepan and add the vanilla bean, then warm over medium heat until just boiling.

Meanwhile, beat the egg yolks, sugar, and cornstarch together in a heatproof bowl until you have a smooth paste.

Gradually pour the hot milk over the egg yolk mixture, stirring constantly (remove the vanilla bean, then rinse, pat dry, and reserve for use in another recipe). Pour the custard mixture into a clean saucepan and cook gently, stirring constantly, until it thickens.

Pour the hot custard over the baked apples just before serving.

Blackberry Butter Crust Pie

SERVES 6

There is something so homey and warm about making a pie. It creates the most wonderful aroma in the kitchen and there is nothing like that familiar taste of buttery crust that I grew up with in Ireland. You can make it with lots of different fruits, such as apples, peaches, strawberries, raspberries, and blueberries. Serve with a big dollop of softly whipped cream.

FOR THE DOUGH

16 tablespoons butter (2 sticks), softened

¼ cup superfine sugar, plus extra for sprinkling

2 eggs, plus 1 egg, beaten, for glazing

grated zest of 1 lemon

2¾ cups all-purpose flour, plus extra for dusting

FOR THE FILLING

2 cups fresh blackberries

¾ cup granulated sugar

1 teaspoon ground cinnamon

grated zest of 1 lemon

whipped cream or vanilla ice cream, to serve

To make the dough, place the butter and sugar in the bowl of a stand mixer or a large bowl and use the paddle attachment on the stand mixer or an electric hand mixer to beat on a high speed until pale and fluffy. Add the 2 eggs and lemon zest and beat for several minutes, then add the flour and mix together on low speed until a dough forms.

Turn the dough onto a floured work surface and form into a ball, then wrap in plastic wrap and chill in the fridge for at least an hour—this will give the crust a crumblier texture once baked.

To make the pie, roll out two-thirds of the dough (keep the remaining dough wrapped in the fridge) on a lightly floured work surface to about ¼-inch thick and use to line a 10-inch ovenproof flat plate, trimming the edges with a knife. Place in the fridge to chill while you wash and drain the blackberries.

Remove the dough-lined plate from the fridge, then top with the blackberries in an even layer and sprinkle with the sugar, cinnamon, and lemon zest.

Roll out the remaining dough on a lightly floured work surface to about ¼-inch thick again and cut it into eight strips. Arrange and weave the dough strips into a lattice pattern on top of the pie, then crimp all the way around the edge with your fingers and thumb to seal and neaten.

Brush the dough all over with the beaten egg and sprinkle with superfine sugar, then chill in the fridge for 30 minutes.

Meanwhile, preheat the oven to 350°F.

Once chilled, bake the pie for about 45 minutes–1 hour until the blackberries are tender. Remove from the oven and then stand on a wire rack to cool for a while.

Serve the pie warm with whipped cream or vanilla ice cream.

Orange, Pistachio & Yogurt Cake

MAKES I CAKE

oil and all-purpose flour, for dusting

½ cup slightly stale white bread crumbs

I cup almond flour

I cup pistachios, chopped

I teaspoon baking powder

4 eggs

¾ cup superfine sugar

½ cup sunflower oil

¾ cup plain yogurt, plus extra to serve

grated zest of I orange

grated zest of I lemon

FOR THE CITRUS SYRUP

juice of I orange

juice of I lemon

½ cup granulated sugar

I star anise

I cinnamon stick

TO DECORATE

½ cup pistachio nuts, coarsely chopped

grated zest of I orange

This is one of my favorite cakes at this time of the year. It's a much needed burst of sunshine and is deliciously light and moist due to the yogurt. You can make a gluten-free version by simply using gluten-free bread crumbs. You can substitute the pistachios with hazelnuts, but roast the hazelnuts before you add them to the cake as it really enhances their flavor. It will last for one week, but I am not sure you will have any left by then!

Preheat the oven to 375°F. Oil an 8-inch round cake pan, 2 inches deep, then lightly dust with flour.

Add the bread crumbs, almond flour, pistachios, and baking powder to a large bowl and mix together.

In a separate bowl, whisk the eggs and superfine sugar together, then gradually pour in the sunflower oil, whisking constantly, followed by the yogurt.

Add the wet mixture to the dry mixture and mix together well, then stir in the orange and lemon zest.

Pour the cake batter into the prepared pan and bake for 45 minutes–1 hour or until golden brown and a skewer inserted into the center comes out clean.

While the cake finishes baking, make the citrus syrup: Place all the ingredients in a saucepan and bring gently to a boil, stirring until the sugar has dissolved completely. Simmer for 10 minutes or until thick.

When the cake is cooked, remove from the oven and let cool in the pan for 5 minutes before turning onto a plate. While the cake is still warm, pierce it several times with a skewer, then spoon the hot syrup over the cake, allowing it to run into the holes. Let the cake cool completely, spooning any excess syrup back over the cake every now and then until it is all soaked up.

Sprinkle with the coarsely chopped pistachios and orange zest to decorate, then serve with extra yogurt.

Vanilla Panna Cotta with Honeyed Figs

SERVES 4

There are so many different flavors and fruits that you can add to this panna cotta. The figs can be swapped for raspberries, blackberries, peaches, or strawberries, or just serve it simply with no fruit at all. I have added lots of different extracts and waters too. Some of my favorites are rosewater, orange blossom water, and lavender extract. I have also infused the panna cotta with different herbs, such as rosemary, lemon thyme, and lemon verbena—all are fabulous!

FOR THE PANNA COTTA

I cup heavy cream

I vanilla bean, slit lengthwise

2 tablespoons superfine sugar

I cup milk

3 gelatin sheets

FOR THE FIGS

2 tablespoons butter, melted

2 tablespoons Irish (or locally sourced) honey

I rosemary sprig, leaves picked and finely chopped

4 ripe figs, quartered

For the panna cotta, pour the cream into a saucepan, add the vanilla bean, and sugar and bring to a boil, stirring until the sugar has dissolved. Reduce the heat and simmer for about 5 minutes until reduced by one-third. Remove the vanilla bean and when cool enough to handle, scrape the softened insides into the cream.

While the cream is reducing, pour the milk into a separate saucepan, add the gelatin sheets, and let soak for about 15 minutes or until soft.

Remove the gelatin and set aside, then heat the milk until boiling, return the gelatin to the milk, and stir until dissolved. Pour the milk and gelatin mixture through a sieve into the hot cream and then pour into four glasses. Let cool completely, cover, and place in the fridge for an hour until set.

For the figs, preheat the oven to 350°F.

Place the melted butter, honey, and rosemary in a shallow baking dish and whisk together. Add the quartered figs and turn to coat with the mixture. Roast for about 15 minutes until the figs are tender and the cooking liquid is syrupy, brushing with the cooking liquid halfway through. Remove from the oven and let cool.

Remove the panna cotta from the fridge about 30 minutes before serving to warm up a little, then spoon the honeyed figs on top of each panna cotta and serve.

Roasted Hazelnut Hot Chocolate Puddings

MAKES 6 INDIVIDUAL PUDDINGS

There's that moment when you spoon into the first bite of a hot chocolate pudding and wait for the delightful gooey chocolate interior to come running out into your spoon—heaven! The trick is not to overcook them as they really don't need more than 8 minutes to bake. Just ensure that your oven is properly preheated. You can make the mixture up a few hours ahead and store it in the fridge. The hazelnuts are so delicious crusted around the top and sides of the pudding—I also swap them with almonds, Brazil nuts, or pistachios. If I have some nice berries, such as raspberries, blueberries, or blackberries, I'll pop a few into the pudding mix too.

2 tablespoons butter

¾ cup blanched hazelnuts, very finely chopped

6 ounces dark chocolate (70% cocoa solids), broken into chunks

4 eggs, separated

½ cup superfine sugar

½ cup all-purpose flour

Preheat the oven to 350°F. Grease six ovenproof china cups or small ramekins with the butter, then sprinkle one-quarter of the finely chopped hazelnuts evenly around the inside of each, setting aside another quarter for topping the puddings.

Melt the chocolate in a heatproof bowl set over a saucepan of simmering water (don't let the bottom of the bowl touch the water).

While the chocolate is melting, in a separate bowl, whisk the egg yolks, sugar, and the remaining hazelnuts together.

Whisk the melted chocolate into the egg yolk mixture, then fold in the flour.

In another very clean and dry bowl, whisk the egg whites until stiff, then gently fold into the chocolate mixture.

Pour the pudding mixture into the prepared cups or ramekins and sprinkle the reserved hazelnuts on top. Stand on a baking sheet and bake in the oven for 9–10 minutes.

Sticky Figgy Cake

MAKES 1 CAKE (SERVES 12)

A true fall hero! I came up with this recipe when I had an abundance of figs from the tree in my garden, and I absolutely love a sticky toffee pudding—so this is a little similar in flavor but much lighter. Make sure you use ripe figs to maximize flavor, and you can leave out the frosting if you wish.

12 dried pitted dates

5½ ounces dried figs

3¾ cups water

16 tablespoons (2 sticks) unsalted butter, softened, plus extra for greasing

1½ cups packed light brown sugar

4 large eggs

2 teaspoons vanilla extract

2½ cups self-rising flour

2 teaspoons baking soda

3 medium-sized fresh figs

FOR THE FROSTING

1½ cups cream cheese, softened

2 cups confectioners' sugar, sifted

TO DECORATE

12 fresh figs, halved

1 orange, for zesting

2 tablespoons Irish (or locally sourced) honey

Preheat the oven to 350°F. Grease a 12-inch springform cake pan.

Place the dates, dried figs, and water in a saucepan over medium heat and bring to a boil. Reduce the heat and simmer for 30 minutes.

Remove the pan from the heat and leave the date and fig mixture to cool for 10 minutes, then transfer to a blender or food processor and blend to a purée. Set aside.

Place the butter and brown sugar in the bowl of a stand mixer or a large bowl and use the paddle attachment on the stand mixer or an electric hand mixer to beat on high speed until pale and fluffy. Add the eggs, one at a time, beating well after each addition, then beat in the vanilla extract. Fold in the flour and baking soda, followed by the date and fig purée.

Pour the cake batter into the greased pan. Slice the fresh figs and place in a fan arrangement on top. Bake for 50–55 minutes or until golden brown and a skewer inserted into the center comes out clean.

Remove the cake from the oven, then release the cake from the pan, transfer to a wire rack, and let cool completely.

Meanwhile, make the frosting: Place the cream cheese and confectioners' sugar in the bowl of the stand mixer or a large bowl and use the paddle attachment or an electric hand mixer to beat together on high speed until well-combined, light, and fluffy.

Spread the frosting on top of the cooled cake. To decorate, arrange the halved figs on the frosting and zest the orange over the top. Lastly, drizzle the honey over the cake.

Banana Cake with Coconut Frosting

MAKES I CAKE

I just love a good banana cake. Make sure you use very ripe bananas—otherwise, you don't get a good banana flavor. The frosting is light and fluffy, producing delicious exotic coconut flavors. You can use this frosting recipe for lots of different cakes and feel free to add different flavors like orange blossom water. Sprinkle raw coconut flakes on top as it adds great texture and looks so pretty... It is also, by the way, a fantastic way to use up bananas that have blackened.

I stick unsalted butter, softened, plus extra for greasing

²/₃ cup light brown sugar

2 eggs

1 ½ cups very ripe bananas, mashed

¼ cup sour cream

½ teaspoon vanilla extract

1 ½ cups all-purpose flour, plus extra for dusting

1 ½ teaspoons baking powder

½ teaspoon baking soda

2 teaspoons ground cinnamon

FOR THE COCONUT FROSTING

¾ cup cream cheese, softened

3 tablespoons unsalted butter, softened

½ cup confectioners' sugar, sifted

3 tablespoons well-stirred coconut cream

FOR THE FILLING

5 tablespoons butter

2 bananas, sliced

¹/₃ cup raw coconut flakes, toasted, to decorate

Preheat the oven to 325°F. Lightly grease a round 10-inch cake pan and dust with flour.

Place the butter and brown sugar in the bowl of a stand mixer or a large bowl and use the paddle attachment on the stand mixer or an electric hand mixer to beat on high speed until pale and fluffy. Add the eggs, one at a time, beating well after each addition, then add the mashed bananas, sour cream, and vanilla extract and beat until well-combined. Sift in the dry ingredients and mix together on low speed.

Spread the cake batter into the prepared pan and bake for 45 minutes or until pale golden and a skewer inserted into the center comes out clean.

Remove the cake from the oven and let cool in the pan for 10 minutes, then transfer the cake from the pan to a wire rack to cool completely.

To make the frosting, place all the ingredients in the bowl of the stand mixer or a bowl and use the paddle attachment or electric hand mixer to beat together on a high speed until well-combined, light, and fluffy. This should take about 2 minutes.

For the filling, place a frying pan over medium heat and add the butter. Once it has melted, add the banana slices and cook until golden brown and caramelized on both sides.

To assemble, slice the cooled cake in half horizontally. Spread half the frosting over the bottom half of the cake and arrange the caramelized bananas on top, then cover with the top half of the cake. Spread the remaining frosting on the top of the cake and sprinkle with the coconut flakes to decorate.

Winter Suppers

Menus

CHRISTMAS DAY

BRUSSELS SPROUT PETAL SALAD

ROSEMARY, CRANBERRY & CLEMENTINE
TURKEY WITH SWEET POTATO, BACON
& PECAN STUFFING

CHOCOLATE PECAN BROWNIE TRIFLE
WITH ORANGE BLOSSOM CREAM

COZY FAMILY SUPPER

KALE, BEAN & WINTER ROOTS SOUP

CORNED BEEF WITH SMASHED TURNIPS
& PARSLEY SAUCE

DATE & ALMOND BREAD & BUTTER
PUDDING

FONDUE NIGHT

CHICKEN LIVER PÂTÉ

WEEKEND FONDUE WITH BREAD
& PICKLES

TARTE TATIN WITH THYME

NEW YEAR'S EVE CELEBRATION

BAKED WHOLE VACHERIN MONT D'OR
WITH ROSEMARY CRISPBREADS

PORK TENDERLOIN FILLED WITH
BUTTERNUT SQUASH & HAZELNUTS
SERVED WITH MASHED CELERY ROOT

PLUM PUDDING ICE CREAM

ONE-POT WINTER SUPPER

BROILED CAULIFLOWER WITH SUMAC
YOGURT, HAZELNUTS & POMEGRANATE

WINTER CHICKEN CASSEROLE

HOT CHOCOLATE AFFOGATO WITH
CANDIED ORANGE PEEL

WINTER GATHERING

CELERY ROOT SOUP WITH HAZELNUT &
SAGE PESTO

BEEF CASSEROLE WITH HERBY
POTATO DUMPLINGS

BLUE CHEESE OAT CHEESECAKE WITH
IRISH HONEY

WINTER SEAFOOD SUPPER

CRAB, BLOOD ORANGE & FENNEL SALAD

FISH PIE WITH DUBLINER CHEESE
RÖSTI TOPPING

STAR ANISE & ORANGE RICE PUDDING

Brussels Sprout Petal Salad

SERVES 4

This is such a refreshing way to serve Brussels sprouts, which are so delicious in a salad. It does take a bit of time to peel off the petals, but you can get this done a day ahead and store them in a bowl covered with damp paper towels in the fridge. I swap out the kale sometimes with green salad leaves like arugula and watercress. The walnuts are delicious in this salad as they go so well with blue cheese, but you could use hazelnuts, almonds, or pine nuts instead. This appetizer is so light and festive and a gorgeous way to start your Christmas or any winter supper. It also works perfectly as a lunch dish.

1 tablespoon olive oil

1 cup diced pancetta

3 cups Brussels sprouts

7 ounces kale

¾ cup walnuts, toasted and chopped

⅔ cup dried cranberries

¾ cup blue cheese, crumbled

FOR THE DRESSING

1 teaspoon Dijon mustard

½ cup extra virgin olive oil

grated zest and juice of 1 lemon

sea salt and freshly ground black pepper

Place a frying pan over medium heat and add the olive oil. Once the oil has warmed, add the pancetta to the pan, increase the heat to high, and cook, tossing, for 2–3 minutes until the pancetta is crispy. Remove the pan from the heat and set aside.

Place a saucepan of water over high heat and bring to a boil.

Meanwhile, prepare the Brussels sprouts by removing and discarding the outer petals, then peel away all the remaining petals and place them in a bowl. Slice the kale into thin strips.

Add the kale strips to the boiling water for 30 seconds, then drain and pat dry with paper towels. Place in the bowl with the Brussels sprout petals.

To make the dressing, place the mustard, extra virgin olive oil, and lemon zest and juice in a small bowl. Season with salt and pepper and whisk together.

Sprinkle the toasted walnuts, dried cranberries, and crispy pancetta into the bowl with the Brussels sprout petals and kale, then crumble the blue cheese on top. Pour the dressing over the salad and toss together well.

Divide between four serving plates or serve in a large bowl.

Baked Whole Vacherin Mont d'Or with Rosemary Crispbreads

SERVES 4

This is my go-to appetizer in the winter when I am a bit pressed for time but want something utterly delicious so my guests don't feel like I'm cheating! The first time I tasted this recipe was at my friend Giana Ferguson's house on Gubbeen Farm in Ireland—she makes the famed Gubbeen cheese. She served this to me in her cozy farmhouse kitchen using her semisoft Gubbeen cheese— I can still remember the sensation of scooping the crunchy, warm bread into the gooey, aromatic cheese and that first mouthful of silky-smooth cheese infused with rosemary and garlic!

FOR THE CRISPBREADS

½ cup warm water

½ teaspoon fast-action dried yeast

1⅔ cups all-purpose flour, plus extra for dusting

2 tablespoons olive oil, plus extra for oiling and brushing

sea salt and freshly ground black pepper

3 rosemary sprigs, leaves picked and finely chopped, plus extra sprigs, to decorate (optional)

FOR THE BAKED CHEESE

1 whole Vacherin Mont d'Or

2 garlic cloves, crushed

1 tablespoon finely chopped rosemary leaves

¼ cup dry white wine

To make the crispbreads, pour the water into a bowl, sprinkle in the yeast, and whisk together well. Leave for 5 minutes until the mixture starts to foam.

Sift the flour into a large bowl and make a well in the center. Pour the yeast mixture into the well and add the olive oil and a sprinkle of salt. Stir together until a dough forms—it should be moist but not sticky.

Transfer the dough to a floured work surface and knead for 10 minutes. Transfer to an oiled bowl, cover with a clean kitchen towel or plastic wrap, and place in a warm, dry spot for an hour.

Preheat the oven to 350°F. Line a large baking sheet with parchment paper (or use two baking sheets). Divide the dough into eight pieces and roll out each piece on a lightly floured work surface into a rectangle measuring about 4 x 10 inches. Transfer to the lined baking sheet. Brush with olive oil and sprinkle with the chopped rosemary and some salt.

Bake for 15 minutes or until crisp and golden. Remove from the oven and let cool on wire racks.

To prepare the cheese, remove the lid from the cheese box. Make several slits in the top of the cheese with a sharp knife and sprinkle with the garlic, rosemary, and white wine. Season with salt and pepper. Place the lid back on the cheese box, sit the box on a baking sheet, and bake for 15 minutes until melted.

To serve, remove the lid from the cheese box and place the box on a wooden serving board, then arrange the crispbreads around the cheese and scatter with some sprigs of rosemary for decoration, if you wish.

Broiled Cauliflower with Sumac Yogurt, Hazelnuts & Pomegranate

SERVES 4

This appetizer is so beautiful to look at—like a flower on a plate with drizzles of sunshine sprinkled on top. It's a very healthy start to your supper and a great vegetarian option as a main course. If you want to make it vegan, then just use coconut yogurt instead of plain yogurt, which is equally delicious. You can swap out the cauliflower for eggplant or zucchini if you wish. The dressing can be made a day ahead and refrigerated.

1 cauliflower

½ cup plain yogurt

1 tablespoon extra virgin olive oil

juice of ½ lemon

2 teaspoons sumac

sea salt and freshly ground black pepper

⅔ cup blanched hazelnuts

seeds of ½ pomegranate (see page 70)

Preheat the broiler to high. Remove the green leaves from the cauliflower, then slice the cauliflower vertically into slices 1-inch thick. Place on a baking sheet and cook under the broiler for 5 minutes on each side.

While the cauliflower is broiling, make the dressing: Place the yogurt, extra virgin olive oil, lemon juice, and sumac in a bowl. Season with salt and pepper and whisk together well.

Place a frying pan over high heat, add the hazelnuts, and lightly toast, shaking the pan frequently to toast the nuts evenly, for 2 minutes. Remove from the pan, leave until cool enough to handle, then coarsely chop.

Place the broiled cauliflower on a sharing platter or divide between four individual plates. Drizzle the sumac yogurt dressing on top, followed by a sprinkle of the chopped hazelnuts and pomegranate seeds.

Kale, Bean & Winter Roots Soup

SERVES 6

My gorgeous friend, florist Nikki Tibbles, has the most beautiful house in the country and I have been lucky enough to spend many weekends there, foraging, cooking, and sharing suppers together. She makes a big batch of soup every weekend with whatever seasonal vegetables she has and packs it up for her busy week back in London. This recipe is inspired by one of her soups. It feels so nourishing during the winter months when we need lots of goodness to protect ourselves from colds. Plus it's absolutely delicious and full of color. Make it in big batches so that you can freeze and use throughout the week.

3 tablespoons olive oil

3 carrots, peeled and cubed

3 parsnips, peeled and cubed

2 celery ribs, cubed

1 onion, diced

2 teaspoons finely chopped rosemary leaves

3 garlic cloves, crushed

sea salt and freshly ground black pepper

4¼ cups hot chicken or vegetable stock

9 ounces cavolo nero (black or Tuscan kale), chopped

2 x 14-ounce cans cannellini beans, rinsed and drained

TO SERVE

½ cup Parmesan cheese, shaved

1 tablespoon finely chopped rosemary leaves

Place a large, heavy-bottomed saucepan or Dutch oven over low heat and pour in the olive oil, then add the carrots, parsnips, celery, onion, rosemary, and garlic. Season with salt and pepper and stir well. Cover the pan with a lid and leave the vegetables to sweat for 15 minutes, stirring every 5 minutes or so.

Stir in the hot stock and bring to a boil, then let cook for 10–15 minutes or until all the vegetables are tender.

Transfer the soup to a blender or food processor, or use an immersion blender, and blend to a smooth consistency.

Return the soup to the saucepan or casserole dish (if necessary). Stir in the cavolo nero and cannellini beans and cook for 3–4 minutes until the kale has wilted and the beans have heated through. Season to taste.

Divide the soup between warmed bowls and sprinkle with the Parmesan cheese shavings and rosemary to serve.

Chicken Liver Pâté

SERVES 10

I started making this pâté about 16 years ago when I had a few stalls at various farmers' markets in Ireland. It is one of my classic recipes that I love to cook about once a month. I store the leftovers in a mason jar so I can dip in and out of it for snacks and lunch. I like to serve it with cucumber pickle and my Spicy Apple Chutney (see page 201) and with thinly sliced sourdough toast. I have so many variations to this recipe but my favorite is adding about ½ cup smoky pancetta and fresh rosemary instead of the thyme. It will store well in the fridge, so you can make this a couple of days ahead.

4 sticks butter (32 tablespoons), softened

1½ pounds chicken livers, cleaned

3 tablespoons brandy

3 garlic cloves, crushed

1 tablespoon thyme leaves

sea salt and freshly ground black pepper

TO SERVE

Spicy Apple Chutney (page 201)

thinly sliced sourdough

Place a frying pan over medium heat and add a pat of the butter. Once the butter has melted, add the chicken livers and cook for about 15 minutes or until thoroughly cooked with no trace of red remaining, stirring occasionally and breaking up the livers with a wooden spoon. Transfer the cooked livers to a blender or food processor.

Add the brandy, garlic, and thyme to the frying pan and deglaze the pan by scraping up all the tiny pieces of meat and juices from the livers with a whisk—the bottom of the pan is where the real flavor is! Add the brandy mixture to the blender or food processor and process until well-blended. Let cool.

Gradually add the remaining butter to the cooled chicken liver mixture and blend until all the butter has been incorporated and you have a silky-smooth consistency.

Transfer the chicken liver pâté to a large dish, cover with plastic wrap, and chill in the fridge for at least 3 hours until set.

Serve the pâté with my apple chutney and rosemary bread (page 203).

Crab, Blood Orange & Fennel Salad

SERVES 2

This salad is like a ray of sunshine in the middle of winter and is perfect as an appetizer or a main course for lunch. I absolutely love blood oranges—buy the small ones as they are much sweeter, and once you slice into them, the vibrant colors will make you instantly smile. The zestiness of the blood orange enhances the crab, and the fennel adds a gentle fragrance. The added crumble of hazelnuts on top brings great texture, but you could also use almonds instead.

½ fennel bulb, halved and very thinly sliced

1 tablespoon extra virgin olive oil

7 ounces cooked white crab meat

1 tablespoon finely chopped dill

2 teaspoons crème fraîche

sea salt and freshly ground black pepper

2 small blood oranges (or 1 large blood orange)

½ cup blanched hazelnuts, toasted and chopped (see page 148)

Add the sliced fennel to a bowl and pour in the extra virgin olive oil to coat. Add the crab meat, dill, and crème fraîche, season with salt and pepper, and toss together.

Thinly slice the whole blood oranges—I leave the skin on when I'm slicing them, as you get a much cleaner cut, then I cut the skin off the slices with a sharp knife.

Divide the crab salad between two plates and arrange the sliced blood oranges on top of the salad, followed by a sprinkle of the chopped toasted hazelnuts. Serve.

Celery Root Soup with Hazelnut & Sage Pesto

SERVES 6

This is my favorite soup to make during the winter months. The flavor of the celery root is celery-like with nutty undertones, and the consistency of the soup is so creamy. The pesto also adds delicious crunchy texture and earthy flavor. You can make it a few days ahead as it freezes really well, so double the recipe when you are making it so you have a batch for a rainy day! I sometimes add a crumble of crispy, smoky pancetta on top with the pesto.

3 tablespoons butter

1 celery root, peeled and chopped

1 celery rib, chopped

1 onion, chopped

²/₃ cup blanched hazelnuts

sea salt and freshly ground black pepper

4¼ cups hot vegetable stock

½ cup crème fraîche

FOR THE HAZELNUT
& SAGE PESTO

²/₃ cup blanched hazelnuts

2 tablespoons finely chopped sage

2 tablespoons extra virgin olive oil

Place a heavy-bottomed saucepan over medium heat and add the butter. Once the butter has melted, add the celery root, celery, onion, and whole hazelnuts, and season with salt and pepper. Stir well, then reduce the heat to low, cover the pan with foil or your butter wrapper, and pop the lid on. Leave the vegetables to sweat for 15 minutes.

Next make the hazelnut and sage pesto: Place a frying pan over high heat, add the hazelnuts, and toast, shaking the pan frequently to toast the nuts evenly, for 3 minutes—this will release all the oils and the flavor.

Add the chopped sage to the extra virgin olive oil in a small bowl.

Put the toasted hazelnuts onto one half of a clean kitchen towel, then fold over the other half of the kitchen towel to cover and bash the nuts with a rolling pin until crushed. Add the crushed nuts to the olive oil and sage, mix together well, and set aside.

Add the hot stock to the vegetables and bring to a boil, then leave to cook, uncovered, for about 15 minutes until the vegetables are tender.

Transfer the soup to a blender or food processor, or use an immersion blender and blend to a smooth consistency.

Return the soup to the saucepan (if necessary). Stir in the crème fraîche and place over medium heat for just 2 minutes to warm through.

Serve the soup in warmed bowls with the hazelnut and sage pesto drizzled on top.

Winter Chicken Casserole

SERVES 4

5 tablespoons butter

1 whole organic or free-range chicken, about 3 pounds, cut into 8 pieces

sea salt and freshly ground black pepper

8 shallots, peeled and left whole

4 carrots, peeled and chopped into 2-inch pieces

2 parsnips, peeled and chopped into 2-inch pieces

4 garlic cloves, peeled and left whole

16 baby potatoes, washed

1 cup dry white wine (optional)

4¼ cups hot chicken stock

grated zest and juice of 1 lemon, leftover lemon reserved

1 tablespoon Irish (or locally sourced) honey

1 tablespoon Dijon mustard

2 flat-leaf parsley sprigs, chopped

4 thyme sprigs

1 sage sprig

2 bay leaves

green leaf salad, to serve

I love to get a big pot of this hearty chicken casserole on in the afternoon or the evening before and then reheat it before serving. The flavors enhance so much if you make it a day ahead, but either way it's a lovely, warming supper dish to serve during the winter. I sometimes add leeks or cherry tomatoes on their vines if I have them. You don't have to use a whole chicken, and I often use chicken thighs or breasts with the bones in them. I say to use chicken stock in the recipe, but I often have a pot of vegetable broth brewing which works just as well. Any leftover chicken is delicious in a chicken salad the next day.

Preheat the oven to 350°F.

Place a Dutch oven over medium heat and add half the butter. Once the butter has melted, add the chicken pieces in batches, skin-side down, and sear over medium-high heat until lightly browned, then season with salt and pepper. Remove from the pot and set aside.

Add the remaining butter to the pot, stir in the shallots, carrots, parsnips, and garlic, and cook until lightly browned.

Return the seared chicken to the pot and stir in the baby potatoes. Pour in the white wine and simmer for 5 minutes to allow the alcohol to evaporate— adding the wine is optional, but it does give a beautiful flavor.

Whisk the stock, lemon zest and juice, honey, and mustard together, then pour into the pot. Slice up the leftover lemon and add to the dish. Lastly, stir in the herbs.

Cover the pot with the lid, transfer to the preheated oven, and cook for 1½ hours.

I like to present this casserole in its dish in the center of the table, and serve my family and friends at the table to create a relaxed atmosphere. Serve with a fresh green leaf salad.

Beef Casserole with Herby Potato Dumplings

1½ pounds boneless stew beef, cut into 2-inch chunks

2½ tablespoons all-purpose flour

sea salt and freshly ground black pepper

5 tablespoons butter

8 shallots, peeled and left whole

1½ cups diced pancetta

2 garlic cloves, crushed

2¾ cups white mushrooms, quartered

⅔ cup whole peeled chestnuts, coarsely chopped

1¾ cups Irish stout

¾ cup hot beef stock

1 teaspoon finely chopped thyme leaves

2 tablespoons grated dark chocolate

FOR THE HERBY POTATO DUMPLINGS

2¼ pounds potatoes, peeled

5 tablespoons butter

2 tablespoons finely chopped flat-leaf parsley

1 tablespoon finely chopped sage

1 tablespoon finely chopped thyme leaves

1⅔ cups all-purpose flour, plus extra for dusting

FOR THE ROUX

3 tablespoons butter

⅓ cup all-purpose flour

The longer you can leave the casserole to cook over low heat the better, as the beef will keep tenderizing. I like to serve slices of roasted butternut squash tossed in olive oil, ground cumin, and garlic as a side dish to this casserole. By the way, the chocolate in this recipe is not a mistake. The French have being doing it for years, and it adds a fabulous rich flavor and velvety texture—you will love it.

Preheat the oven to 275°F. Place the beef in a large bowl, sprinkle with the flour, and season with salt and pepper. Toss to coat.

Place a Dutch oven over medium heat and melt half the butter. Add all the beef and cook, stirring occasionally, for about 5 minutes until browned. Transfer the beef to a bowl.

Add the shallots and pancetta to the pot and cook for 5 minutes. Increase the heat to get the pancetta really crispy and the shallots golden brown. Transfer the shallots and pancetta to the same bowl as the beef. Add the remaining butter to the pot, then stir in the garlic, mushrooms, and chestnuts and cook for 3 minutes.

Return all the browned ingredients to the casserole dish, pour in the stout and stock, and stir in the thyme and chocolate. Bring to a boil, then cover the casserole dish with the lid, transfer to the oven, and cook for 1 hour.

Meanwhile, make the dumplings: Place the potatoes in a saucepan and fill halfway with water. Cover with a lid and bring to a boil, then reduce the heat and simmer for 30–35 minutes or until the potatoes are completely cooked.

Drain the potatoes and transfer to a bowl. Season, add the butter and finely chopped herbs, and mash well. Add the flour and stir to combine. Dust your hands with flour, then shape the potato and herb mixture into dumplings slightly smaller in size than a tennis ball. You should be able to make six.

Before you add the dumplings to the stew, make the roux: Once the casserole has cooked for an hour, remove from the oven. Melt the butter in a small saucepan over medium heat, stir in the flour, then gradually strain all the liquid from the casserole into the roux, whisking constantly, and cook until the sauce is thick and smooth. Pour the sauce back into the casserole.

Arrange the herby potato dumplings on top of the stew so that it is completely covered, return to the oven without the lid, and bake for 35 minutes. Serve.

Corned Beef with Smashed Turnips & Parsley Sauce

SERVES 6

On cold winter evenings in London when I miss home, I make my way to the local butcher and get myself a salt-cured silverside of beef. Once I am back in my kitchen, I get the beef cooking and turn it into what we call corned beef, very similar to the Jewish salted beef. Served with buttery golden turnips and creamy peppery parsley sauce, this is my Irish comfort food that makes me so happy.

2¼ pounds salt-cured silverside beef

2 bay leaves

1 onion, chopped

FOR THE TURNIPS

14 ounces turnips, peeled and chopped (about 3 cups)

3 tablespoons butter

sea salt and freshly ground black pepper

FOR THE PARSLEY SAUCE

2 tablespoons butter

1 onion, finely diced

2 tablespoons all-purpose flour

¾ cup milk

2 tablespoons finely chopped curly parsley

1 teaspoon English mustard

pinch of freshly grated nutmeg

Place the beef, bay leaves, and onion in a large saucepan, cover with water, and bring to a boil over high heat. Reduce to a simmer and skim off the foam that accumulates on the surface of the water. Cover the pan with a lid and simmer for about 2½ hours or until the beef is tender.

Remove the beef from its cooking liquid, wrap in foil, and set aside. Reserve about 1¾ cups of the cooking liquid.

For the turnips, place them in a saucepan with half the reserved beef cooking liquid. Bring to a boil, then reduce the heat and simmer for 20 minutes or until tender.

Drain the turnips and return to the pan. Add the butter and season with salt and pepper. Smash the turnips coarsely using a potato masher.

To make the parsley sauce, melt the butter in a saucepan over medium heat. Stir in the onion and cook for 1 minute, then stir in the flour and cook, stirring, for about another minute. Add the remaining reserved beef cooking liquid, the milk, parsley, mustard, and nutmeg, and season with salt and pepper. Continue to whisk until you have a smooth consistency. Cook for another 3 minutes, whisking constantly, until the sauce thickens.

To serve, slice the beef against the grain onto a warmed platter and spoon the smashed turnips alongside. Pour the parsley sauce into a warmed bowl and then over the meat when you are ready to serve.

Rosemary, Cranberry & Clementine Turkey with Sweet Potato, Bacon & Pecan Stuffing

SERVES 8

1 organic or free-range turkey, 9–10 pounds

Sweet Potato, Bacon & Pecan Stuffing (see page 165)

sea salt and freshly ground black pepper

FOR THE FLAVORED BUTTER

10 tablespoons salted butter, softened

2/3 cup dried cranberries, very finely chopped

4 rosemary sprigs, leaves picked and finely chopped

grated zest of 1 clementine, then fruit peeled, segmented, and chopped

FOR THE ROASTING PAN

4 shallots, peeled and halved

3 carrots, peeled and cut into 3-inch pieces

1 garlic bulb, halved through the middle

4 small bunches of thyme

4 small bunches of sage

2 clementines, halved

The clementines and cranberries are so festive, and together with the fresh rosemary, they pack lots of delicious flavors into the turkey. I love dressing the turkey platter with slices of clementines and sprigs of fresh rosemary. Do make sure you take the turkey out of the fridge at least an hour before you put it in the oven, as it will give you a more tender result. You can dress the turkey in the flavored butter a day ahead and use it for a turkey crown or leg also.

If you are using a frozen turkey, it is best to defrost the bird in the fridge. It will need about 24 hours to defrost for every 4½ pounds. Take the turkey out of the fridge an hour before roasting to allow the meat to relax and come to room temperature, which will make the meat more tender.

Meanwhile, preheat the oven to 450°F. Remove the giblets from inside the bird's cavity because these can't be cooked with the turkey. Keep them for making turkey stock or gravy. Season the cavity with salt and pepper.

Place all the ingredients for the flavored butter in a bowl, season with salt and pepper, and mix well, using the back of a spoon to blend the ingredients together. Using clean hands, smear the butter mixture all over the turkey as well as underneath the skin.

Add the stuffing to the cavity of the turkey, ensuring that it is only half-filled to allow hot air to circulate and the turkey to cook more evenly.

Line the roasting pan first with the shallots, carrots, garlic, thyme, sage, and clementines, then place the stuffed turkey on top. This will flavor the turkey even more during the roasting process.

Roast the turkey for 45 minutes, then reduce the oven temperature to 350°F, remove the turkey from the oven, and baste the bird with the juices from the pan. Cover the turkey loosely with foil, return to the oven, and roast for 3½ hours, continuing to baste the turkey every 45 minutes.

Check to see if the turkey is cooked by inserting a skewer into the thickest part of the thigh—the juices should run clear. Once you have removed the turkey from the oven, let it rest for 30 minutes, covered with a loose tent of foil to keep it warm, before carving and serving. This will allow the juices to redistribute themselves, resulting in tastier meat.

Sweet Potato, Bacon & Pecan Stuffing

SERVES 8

3 tablespoons salted butter

½ cup thick-cut bacon, chopped

1 small onion, finely diced

2 celery ribs, finely diced

2 garlic cloves, crushed

1¾ cups sweet potatoes, diced

2 tablespoons maple syrup

2¾ cups fresh white bread crumbs

½ cup pecans, chopped

⅓ cup dried cranberries

½ cup hot chicken or turkey stock

2 teaspoons finely chopped thyme leaves

sea salt and freshly ground black pepper

If you want to cook the stuffing separately from the turkey, preheat the oven to 350°F.

Place a saucepan over medium heat and add the butter. Once the butter has melted, stir in the bacon and cook for 2 minutes, then add the onion, celery, and garlic and cook for another 3 minutes. Stir in the sweet potatoes and maple syrup and cook for another 2–3 minutes.

Place the bread crumbs in a baking dish, followed by the pecans, dried cranberries, stock, and thyme, and season with salt and pepper. Add the sweet potato mixture and mix all the ingredients until well-combined.

Bake the stuffing for 30 minutes until well-browned on top.

Pork Tenderloin Filled with Butternut Squash & Hazelnuts served with Mashed Celery Root

SERVES 4

I love pork loins—they are so easy to cook and work with. In the fall, I also use blackberries, and substitute apples for the butternut squash. You can use this filling for a bigger piece of pork—just double the recipe. And you can get this all prepared a day ahead so it's a really great stress-free main course.

FOR THE STUFFING

14 ounces butternut squash, peeled, seeded, and diced (about 2¾ cups)

½ cup blanched hazelnuts, finely chopped

1 red onion, finely diced

6 sage leaves, finely chopped

¼ cup fresh white bread crumbs

3 tablespoons butter, melted

2 garlic cloves, crushed

sea salt and ground black pepper

FOR THE PORK

14-ounce pork tenderloin

8 pancetta slices or bacon

butter, for greasing

FOR THE CELERY ROOT

1½ pounds celery root, peeled and cut into chunks (4½ cups)

½ cup half-and-half

3 tablespoons butter

½ teaspoon freshly grated nutmeg

Preheat the oven to 400°F.

Start by making the stuffing: Place all the ingredients in a large bowl, season with salt and pepper, and mix together well.

Butterfly the pork tenderloin by making a slit down its length, cutting just deep enough so that you can open the loin up to lie flat like a book; don't cut all the way through.

Arrange the pancetta or bacon side by side on a lightly greased, large baking sheet, then place the pork on top. Spoon the stuffing mixture onto the meat and spread evenly. Close up the tenderloin bit by bit by stretching the pancetta or bacon and using it to wrap around and seal the pork, working all the way along its length so that you end up with a big package.

Roast the pork for 25 minutes.

While the pork finishes roasting, make the mashed celery root: Place the celery root in a saucepan and cover with cold water. Bring to a boil over high heat, then reduce to a simmer and cook for 15 minutes or until the celery root is tender.

Add the half-and-half, butter, and nutmeg to a saucepan and warm together over low heat. Pour the cream mixture over the cooked celery root, season with salt and pepper, and mash together.

Once the pork is cooked, remove from the oven and let rest for 15 minutes, tented with foil to keep it warm. Slice the pork and place on a warmed platter, then spoon the mashed celery root around the pork.

Weekend Fondue with Bread & Pickles

SERVES 4

Cheese fondue is such a fun dish to share with friends and family, especially during the winter months since it is so warming. I love to serve this in the middle of the table in my big Le Creuset casserole dish that I have had for years, but if you have a proper fondue set, all the better. Dipping in pickles and chunks of bread to scoop up the melting silky cheese is utter winter heaven!

1¼ cups dry white wine

2 garlic cloves, finely chopped

2¾ cups Emmental cheese, grated

4½ cups good-quality Gruyère cheese, grated

5½ ounces Reblochon cheese

2 teaspoons kirsch (optional)

whole nutmeg, for grating

TO SERVE

sourdough bread, cubed

pickles, such as pickled gherkins, onions, and cucumbers

Heat the wine with the garlic in a deep, heavy-bottomed saucepan over low heat until it begins to simmer.

Add the Emmental, a little at a time, whisking or stirring vigorously and leaving it to melt after each addition before adding more. Repeat the process with the Gruyère, followed by the Reblochon, continuing to stir until smooth.

Stir in the kirsch, if using, followed by a good grating of nutmeg.

Transfer the fondue mixture to a fondue set or heatproof pan set over a tea light and serve with sourdough bread cubes and pickles.

Fish Pie with Dubliner Cheese Rösti Topping

SERVES 2

This is the ultimate fish pie—I promise you! I cook regularly on the UK's *Sunday Brunch*, and last winter I cooked this dish. I was inundated with viewers sending me their pictures of this fish pie from their kitchens at home, so this is definitely my most celebrated TV recipe to date! The smoky, creamy base of the pie topped with the crispy potato and cheese rösti on top is the perfect texture combination. You can get the crust made a day ahead, and then prepare the rösti on the day. Also feel free to swap out the fish for any meaty fish that you like and leave out the cheese in the potato rösti if you prefer.

1 pound Idaho or Russet potatoes

2 ounces aged Dubliner cheese

9 ounces skinless smoked haddock fillet

9 ounces skinless salmon fillet

3½ ounces raw, peeled shrimp

1¾ cups whole milk

1 shallot, peeled and halved

1 bay leaf

1 teaspoon black peppercorns

5 tablespoons butter, softened

⅓ cup all-purpose flour

2 teaspoons Dijon mustard

sea salt and freshly ground black pepper

2 tablespoons chopped dill

Preheat the oven to 400°F.

Peel the potatoes, then grate using the large holes on a box grater. Place the grated potatoes in a bowl of cold water to stop them from turning brown.

Grate the cheese using the same side of the grater and set aside separately—you should have about ½ cup.

Place the smoked haddock, salmon, and shrimp in a saucepan, pour in the milk, and drop in the shallot, bay leaf, and peppercorns. Cook over low heat for 5 minutes, then drain, reserving the poaching milk but discarding the onion, bay leaf, and peppercorns. Transfer the fish to a baking dish.

Melt 3 tablespoons of the butter in a saucepan over medium heat. Stir in the flour and cook, continuing to stir, until a paste (roux) forms. Gradually add the reserved fish poaching milk as well as the mustard, whisking constantly, and cook until you have a smooth, thickened sauce. Season with salt and pepper and stir in half the dill, then pour the sauce over the fish.

Drain the grated potatoes and pat with a clean kitchen towel until they are completely dry. Mix the grated potatoes and the remaining dill into the grated cheese and season with salt, then scatter over the fish and the sauce.

Melt the remaining butter in a saucepan and brush over the top of the pie to ensure that the top gets really crispy. Bake for 20 minutes or until golden brown.

Plum Pudding Ice Cream

SERVES 6

Making your own ice cream is so simple—it really is just a matter of placing all the ingredients in a pot over low heat, stirring, freezing, and whisking every hour or so. You don't need an ice cream maker. Adding the crumbles of plum pudding gives delicious little surprise bits of juicy fruitiness. It's a light and refreshing dessert to serve during the Christmas period and also a great way to use up any leftover pudding from the holidays. The grated zest of an orange would also be a lovely addition.

1 cup heavy cream

1 cup whole milk

¾ cup superfine sugar

1 vanilla bean

5 egg yolks

1 cup plum pudding, crumbled

Pour the cream and milk into a saucepan, place over medium heat, and stir in the sugar. Slit the vanilla bean down its length with a small sharp knife, scoop out the tiny black seeds, and stir into the saucepan. Reduce the heat and stir until all the sugar has dissolved, then remove the pan from the heat.

Place the eggs yolks in a large bowl and beat to combine, then slowly whisk in the warmed cream and milk mixture. Return the mixture to the saucepan, place over low heat, and stir until it thickens to a custard consistency.

Remove the pan from the heat, pour the ice cream mixture into a freezerproof container, and let cool completely.

Freeze the ice cream mixture for 2 hours, then remove from the freezer and stir well with a fork until you have a smooth consistency (this will prevent any ice crystals from forming). Return to the freezer for 30 minutes and then repeat the stirring process. Freeze for another 30 minutes, then fold in ½ cup of the crumbled plum pudding (reserve the remainder for serving) and return to the freezer for a final 2 hours of freezing.

Serve the ice cream with the remaining crumble of plum pudding on top.

Hot Chocolate Affogato with Candied Orange Peel

SERVES 4

When I lived in Italy, affogato was something I served for dessert all the time. It's everything you want in a dessert—refreshing chilled ice cream warmed with hot espresso coffee. This version is a bit more special with the rich, silky, melted dark chocolate and the festive fresh flavor of orange. It's one of the easiest desserts to make and it looks and tastes fantastic!

¾ cup heavy cream

7 ounces dark chocolate (70% cocoa solids), chopped (or use nibs)

½ cup strong espresso coffee

grated zest of 1 orange

8 scoops of good-quality vanilla ice cream

8 strips of candied orange peel

Place the cream, dark chocolate, espresso, and orange zest in a saucepan over low heat. Heat, stirring, until the chocolate has melted into the cream.

Add two scoops of vanilla ice cream to four chilled glasses and place each on a saucer along with a spoon and two strips of candied orange peel. Pour the chocolate and espresso sauce into a warmed serving container.

Bring everything to the table and assemble the affogato in front of everyone, as the ice cream will melt once you pour over the sauce, and it looks great too! Arrange two strips of candied orange peel on top of each serving and pour the hot chocolate and espresso sauce over the ice cream.

Blue Cheese Oat Cheesecake with Irish Honey

MAKES 1 CHEESECAKE

Blue cheese is at its best during the winter months, and I think we all love smoky creamy cheese around this time of the year. If you're not a fan of blue cheese, you can make this dish with cream cheese, but if you are doing so then I would leave out the thyme. The blue cheese together with the earthy flavor of the fresh thyme, sweetened by the honey and a base of crunchy oatcakes (find these online) is absolutely delicious! You can make this a few days ahead and it will last about a week in the fridge. But take it out of the fridge at least an hour before serving so it comes to room temperature.

7 ounces oatcakes

½ cup walnuts, toasted

7 tablespoons butter, melted, plus extra for greasing

2 cups cream cheese

½ cup sour cream

3 eggs, lightly beaten

⅓ cup all-purpose flour, seasoned

1¾ cups Cashel Blue cheese, or other blue cheese, crumbled

1 tablespoon chopped thyme leaves

2 teaspoons Irish (or locally sourced) honey, plus extra to serve

sea salt and freshly ground black pepper

Preheat the oven to 275°F. Grease and line the bottom and sides of an 8-inch springform cake pan with parchment paper.

Add the oatcakes and toasted walnuts to a food processor and process to crumbs. Transfer to a bowl, add the melted butter with a pinch of salt and a grinding of pepper, and mix together well. Transfer the buttery crumbs to the prepared pan, using the back of a spoon to spread and press them into an even, well-compacted layer over the bottom and sides. Chill in the fridge for at least 30 minutes until firm and cold.

To make the filling, beat the cream cheese in a bowl with a wooden spoon until smooth. Add the sour cream and beat again. Gradually pour in the beaten eggs, beating after each addition, until fully combined.

Sift the seasoned flour over the cream cheese mixture and gently fold it in, then fold in the blue cheese, thyme, and honey until well-combined.

Scrape the mixture into the chilled oatcake crust and smooth the top. Bake for 1 hour or until just set with the tiniest wobble in the center. Turn off the heat and let the cheesecake cool completely in the oven. Serve with a drizzle of extra honey.

Chocolate Pecan Brownie Trifle with Orange Blossom Cream

MAKES 1 TRIFLE

FOR THE CHOCOLATE
BROWNIES

10½ ounces good-quality dark
chocolate (70% cocoa solids),
broken into chunks

7 tablespoons butter, chopped,
plus extra for greasing

4 eggs

1 cup light muscovado or
brown sugar

1½ cups all-purpose flour

1 cup pecans, coarsely chopped

FOR THE CHOCOLATE
MOUSSE

9 ounces good-quality dark
chocolate (70% cocoa solids),
broken into chunks

2 tablespoons cocoa powder

½ cup half-and-half

2 tablespoons orange blossom
water

6 egg whites

½ cup superfine sugar

TO FINISH THE TRIFLE

2 cups heavy whipping cream

1 tablespoon orange blossom
water

½ cup pecans, chopped

2 ounces dark chocolate curls
or flakes

This is a showstopping dessert to serve at Christmas or on special occasions. I always slightly underbake the brownies because they can become dry really fast—you can also swap out the pecans for hazelnuts or almonds if you wish. If you haven't ever used orange blossom water before, please go and buy a bottle—it adds such a magical, delicate floral flavor to any cream. You can serve this in individual glasses or in a large glass trifle bowl. Add soft berries to the top if you wish.

Start by making the brownies: Preheat the oven to 350°F. Grease an 8 x 12-inch baking pan.

Melt the chocolate and butter in a heatproof bowl set over a saucepan of simmering water, stirring gently until smooth and combined (don't let the bottom of the bowl touch the water). Set aside to cool slightly.

Place the eggs and brown sugar in a large bowl or the bowl of a stand mixer and whisk together until pale and fluffy. Whisk the chocolate and butter mixture into the egg mixture, then gently fold in the flour and chopped pecans.

Pour the mixture into the pan, smooth the surface, then bake for 25 minutes or until firm around the edges but slightly soft in the middle. Let cool in the pan for 10 minutes, then turn onto a wire rack to cool completely.

While the brownies are cooling, make the chocolate mousse: Melt the chocolate in a heatproof bowl set over a pan of simmering water (don't let the bottom of the bowl touch the water). Once melted, stir in the cocoa, then remove from the heat and stir in the half-and-half and orange blossom water.

Place the egg whites in a very clean and dry large bowl or the bowl of the stand mixer and use an electric hand mixer or the whisk attachment on the stand mixer to whisk until firm peaks form. Gradually add the sugar, a tablespoon at a time, whisking constantly until the mixture is stiff. Gently fold it into the cooled chocolate mixture.

To finish the trifle, pour the whipping cream into a bowl, add the orange blossom water, and whisk together until softly whipped.

To assemble the trifle, break the brownie into pieces and add half to your trifle bowl. Then spoon half the chocolate mousse on top, followed by half the orange blossom cream. Repeat with the remaining brownie, mousse, and cream, then sprinkle the chopped pecans and chocolate curls or flakes on top.

Tarte Tatin with Thyme

SERVES 6

I experimented with this recipe so many times in my little kitchen in London to get the perfect result. It's such an easy recipe to make, but you need to follow the steps to make it perfectly. Cook the caramel until it is light golden and then immediately place the apples on top followed by the puff pastry, and then put it straight into the oven. You can make it a few hours ahead and just let it sit on the side, then reheat it in a low oven. I love to serve mine with a dollop of crème fraîche. Try swapping out the apples for plums, pears, or peaches at other times of the year.

¾ cup superfine sugar

½ cup water

4 tablespoons unsalted butter

2 teaspoons chopped thyme leaves, plus 6 sprigs, to decorate

4 sweet apples, peeled, cored, and quartered

3 sheets of store-bought puff pastry, defrosted if frozen

crème fraîche, to serve

Preheat the oven to 350°F.

Place a cast iron or ovenproof frying pan over low heat, add the sugar and water, and heat, stirring, until the sugar has dissolved.

Increase the heat to high and simmer for 12–14 minutes or until the syrup is a light golden brown color, then stir in the butter and chopped thyme and cook for another 2–3 minutes or until you have a caramel consistency.

Arrange the apples cut-side up in the pan and slightly overlapping to ensure that the caramel is completely covered with the apples.

Place the puff pastry sheets on top of each other and roll out so that they combine and are large enough to cover the apples in the pan, with enough excess to tuck in around the sides of the pan.

Place the pastry on top of the apples and fold the edges downward to tuck in the apples, then use a sharp knife to make three small slits in the center of the pastry top.

Transfer the pan to the oven and bake for 45 minutes until the pastry is golden brown.

Remove the pan from the oven. Wearing oven mitts, carefully invert the tart onto your serving dish. Cut into wedges, decorate each serving with a thyme sprig, and serve with a dollop of crème fraîche.

Star Anise & Orange Rice Pudding

SERVES 6

Creamy rice pudding infused with the aniseed flavor of star anise and given sweetness and zestiness by the orange is a delicious spoonful of flavor and texture. There are so many variations that I make to this recipe—you can add dried fruit, such as raisins, golden raisins, dates, apricots, or cranberries with a sprinkle of ground cinnamon for a very festive dessert. You can serve it warm, at room temperature, or chilled—all are equally good. If you make it a day ahead, then loosen it up before serving in a saucepan with some warmed milk and stir until the consistency is smooth again.

2 teaspoons butter

1/3 cup pudding (short-grain) rice

1/4 cup superfine sugar

2/3 cup golden raisins

3 star anise

1 teaspoon freshly grated nutmeg

3 1/3 cups milk

grated zest and juice of 1 orange

3 satsumas, peeled and segmented

Preheat the oven to 325°F. Grease a 1.2-quart baking dish with the butter.

Place the rice, sugar, golden raisins, star anise, and nutmeg in the greased baking dish and mix together well. Add the milk and orange zest and juice and stir to mix.

Bake the rice pudding for 1½ hours, stirring a couple of times during the cooking time—a skin will form on the top of the pudding while baking.

Remove the rice pudding from the oven. Scrape back the skin and remove the star anise, then rinse and dry them, cut in half, and use for decorating your puddings.

Fill six glasses one-third of the way with the rice pudding and top with satsuma segments, then repeat the layers until you have filled each glass. Alternatively, you can layer the rice pudding and satsumas in the same way in a large dessert bowl. Decorate with the star anise and serve at room temperature.

Date & Almond Bread & Butter Pudding

SERVES 6

Bread and butter pudding is a childhood favorite of mine. My mother would make it using up all the leftover bread. Now I keep save bread to use for the pudding! You can make this with brioche too, which is a much richer result. The dates and almonds get blended together to make a natural, nutty caramel paste that gets whipped into the eggy milk mixture. In the oven it becomes soufflé-like because of the eggs and milk—so it's fluffy and delicious. Serve with a dollop of softly whipped cream and a dusting of ground cinnamon if you like.

I cup milk

I cup half-and-half

½ cup superfine sugar

4 eggs

I teaspoon vanilla extract

I tablespoon ground cinnamon

14 ounces dried pitted dates (about 16 dates)

½ cup water

12 slices of white bread, cut into triangles

7 tablespoons butter, softened

½ cup blanched almonds, finely chopped

softly whipped cream or ice cream, to serve

Preheat the oven to 325°F.

Place a saucepan over medium heat, add the milk, half-and-half, and sugar, and mix together. Heat, stirring, until the sugar has dissolved, then set aside to cool.

Whisk the eggs in a large bowl, then stir in the vanilla extract and cinnamon. Whisk into the cooled milk mixture.

Place the dates in a blender or food processor with the water and blend to a purée. Then add the date mixture to the custard mixture and mix together.

Spread the triangles of bread with the butter. Arrange them, overlapping, in a baking dish, then pour over the date and custard mixture. Use your hands to push the bread gently into the custard mixture so that it is completely immersed.

Scatter the chopped almonds over the top of the pudding, then bake for 45 minutes. Serve with softly whipped cream or ice cream.

Cocktails, Snacks & Afters

Sparkling Rhubarb Cocktail

This is such a pretty-looking cocktail and one I love to serve before suppers or at a party when the first of the rhubarb comes into season. Make the rhubarb syrup the day before and decant into a pretty glass pitcher alongside a bottle of chilled sparkling wine on a tray with glasses. I like to set this up in the garden on a table with flowers alongside one of my snacks to create a lovely occasion.

SERVES 8

1¾ cups rhubarb, trimmed and chopped

¾ cup superfine sugar

grated zest and juice of 1 orange

chilled sparkling wine, to top off

To make the rhubarb syrup, place the rhubarb, sugar, and orange zest and juice in a saucepan and add a splash of water. Bring to a boil, then reduce the heat to low and simmer gently, uncovered, for 10–15 minutes until the rhubarb is very soft.

Strain the syrup into a pitcher, pressing the rhubarb to extract all the juice, then let cool.

Pour a little of the rhubarb syrup into each glass and top off with chilled sparkling wine.

Fig Leaf & Thyme Cocktail

SERVES 12

FOR THE FIG LEAF & THYME SYRUP

1¾ cups superfine sugar

2 cups water

8 fresh fig leaves, thoroughly washed

8 thyme sprigs

FOR THE COCKTAIL

6 lemons, halved, for squeezing

20 ounces gin

1 quart soda water

ice cubes, to serve

The leaves from the fig tree that I have in my garden flop over the entrance to the house, so I am welcomed by them every day in the summer and fall. There is a lovely soft figgy smell to them, so one day I decided to make a syrup with them along with a little thyme, also from my garden. The result was this wonderful figgy aromatic syrup that is so delicious in this cocktail.

To make the fig leaf and thyme syrup, place the sugar and measured water in a saucepan over high heat and stir until the sugar has dissolved. Stir in the fig leaves and thyme sprigs, reduce the heat, and simmer, uncovered, for 1 hour.

Strain the syrup into a pitcher, discard the fig leaves and thyme, and let cool.

For the cocktail, place a couple of ice cubes in each glass, followed by the juice of ½ lemon. Then pour in a double measure (2 ounces) of gin, 3 tablespoons of the fig leaf and thyme syrup, and ½ cup soda water. Stir and serve.

The Smoky

SERVES 2 (WITH A
TOP-OFF FOR BOTH!)

4 ounces Irish whiskey

4 dashes of Angostura bitters

juice of 1 lemon

juice of ½ orange

5 tablespoons sugar syrup

2 organic or free-range egg
whites

ice cubes

2 orange slices, to garnish
(optional)

My boyfriend and I decided we wanted to create a house cocktail—one that we
would go back to in between seasons and that our friends could look forward to
having when they came for supper. It was a fun weekend experimenting with this
cocktail, full of lots of testing and laughing... We often just make it for ourselves
on a Friday night after a long work week, followed by a little dance! It's similar
to an Old Fashioned—I love the egg white in it as it lightens it all up and gives
a delicious creamy texture. It is my all-time favorite cocktail and has become a
signature drink at all my suppers at home.

Place the whiskey, Angostura bitters, lemon and orange juices, sugar syrup,
and egg whites in a cocktail shaker with some ice cubes. Shake for 1 minute.

Pour into two chilled coupe glasses, then garnish each with an orange slice.

Lime, Mint & Sea Salt Cocktail

SERVES 6

FOR THE LIME & MINT SYRUP

1½ cups superfine sugar

3 cups water

6 mint sprigs, plus 6 half sprigs
to serve

grated zest of 4 limes

FOR THE SODA

juice of 4 limes, plus 2 wedges
and 6 slices to serve

gin

soda water

sea salt and ice, to serve

This is my version of a mojito—salty, sweet, refreshingly cooling with mint, and
zesty from the fresh limes. The syrup is so simple to make, and will last in an
airtight container for up to two weeks, so you can make it well ahead.

To make the lime and mint syrup, place all the ingredients in a saucepan
over medium heat and gently bring to a boil, stirring until the sugar
has dissolved.

Remove the pan from the heat and leave the syrup to infuse for 1 hour.

For the soda, strain the syrup into a pitcher, discard the mint, and stir in the
lime juice.

When you are ready to serve, spread a layer of sea salt on a saucer. Run a lime
wedge around the outside of the rim of each glass and then roll the rim in the
sea salt so that it is completely covered. First fill each glass halfway with ice
and add a lime slice and half a mint sprig. Then fill the glasses one-quarter
of the way with the lime and mint mixture, one-quarter with gin, and the
remaining half with soda water. Stir and serve.

Rosemary & Lemon Gin Soda

SERVES 6

FOR THE ROSEMARY & LEMON SYRUP

1¼ cups superfine sugar

1¼ cups water

3 rosemary sprigs, plus 6, to serve

FOR THE SODA

juice of 6 lemons

gin

soda water

ice cubes and 6 lemon slices, to serve

This cocktail is best served in small tumbler glasses with a thin slice of lemon and a sprig of fresh rosemary, which can also be used as a stirrer. You can serve a non-alcoholic option by just leaving out the gin and adding extra soda water. It's also great with vodka.

To make the rosemary and lemon syrup, place the syrup ingredients in a saucepan over medium heat and gently bring to a boil, stirring until the sugar has dissolved.

Remove the pan from the heat and leave the syrup to infuse for 2 hours.

For the soda, strain the syrup into a pitcher, discard the rosemary, and stir in the lemon juice.

When you are ready to serve, fill each glass halfway with ice cubes and add a lemon slice and a rosemary sprig. Fill the glasses one-quarter of the way with the rosemary and lemon mixture, one-quarter with gin, and the remaining half with soda water. Stir and serve.

Blackberry & Rosemary Cocktail

SERVES 8

FOR THE BLACKBERRY SYRUP

1 cup superfine sugar

2 cups water

1 pound fresh blackberries, plus 8, to serve

FOR THE COCKTAIL

½ cup fresh lemon juice

gin

soda water

ice and 8 rosemary sprigs, to serve

When blackberries are in season, there is nothing more special than spending the weekend foraging for them. There are so many fun things to make from them—this cocktail being one. The blackberry syrup is delicious with fresh rosemary, but you could also use fresh mint. Vodka works well too, and it's also a great non-alcoholic cocktail—just add more soda and leave out the alcohol.

To make the blackberry syrup, place the syrup ingredients in a saucepan over medium heat and gently bring to a boil, stirring until the sugar has dissolved. Remove the pan from the heat and leave the syrup to cool.

Stir the lemon juice into the cooled blackberry syrup.

When you are ready to serve, fill each glass halfway with ice and add a rosemary sprig and a blackberry. Fill the glasses one-quarter of the way with the blackberry and lemon juice mixture, one-quarter with gin, and the remaining half with soda water. Stir and serve.

Butternut Squash & Harissa Hummus

SERVES 6

14 ounces butternut squash, peeled, seeded, and cut into chunks (about 2¾ cups)

3 garlic cloves, unpeeled

sea salt and ground black pepper

½ cup water

3 tablespoons tahini paste

2 tablespoons olive oil, plus extra for drizzling

1 tablespoon harissa, plus extra for drizzling

1 x 14-ounce can chickpeas, rinsed and drained

TO SERVE

2 wedges of lemon

1 teaspoon pumpkin seeds

I came up with this recipe for a Thanksgiving special on *The Marilyn Denis Show*. You can serve this with toasted sourdough, vegetable crudités, or spiced pita breads. To make the spice for the pita, whisk together 2 teaspoons of smoked paprika with the juice of ½ lemon, ¼ cup olive oil, and a sprinkle of sea salt. Cut the pitas into small triangles and brush them with the paprika oil, then transfer onto a baking sheet and into a hot oven for 6–7 minutes until they are toasted.

Preheat the oven to 350°F.

Place the butternut squash chunks and whole garlic cloves in a roasting pan, season well with salt and pepper, and add the water. Cover the pan with foil and bake for about 45 minutes until the squash is tender. Remove from the oven and let cool.

Squeeze the roasted garlic from their skins into a blender or food processor along with the squash and any juices from the roasting pan. Add all the remaining ingredients, season with salt, and blend to a paste.

Scrape the hummus into a bowl. Drizzle with extra harissa, olive oil, and pumpkin seeds. Serve with a couple of lemon wedges on the side.

Tuscan White Bean & Rosemary Dip

SERVES 4

14-ounce can cannellini beans, rinsed and drained

5 tablespoons extra virgin olive oil

1 teaspoon finely chopped rosemary leaves

1 garlic clove, crushed

juice of 1 lemon

1 teaspoon cayenne pepper

sea salt and freshly ground black pepper

vegetable crudités or breadsticks, to serve

A great handy dip recipe to have up your sleeve as it uses mainly pantry ingredients and takes less than 5 minutes to make! When I am serving it, I like to add a sprinkle of chopped toasted almonds on top, a good drizzle of extra virgin olive oil, and some finely chopped fresh rosemary—it adds great texture and it looks so beautiful. You can make this up a day ahead and keep it in the fridge.

Place all the ingredients in a blender or food processor, season with salt and pepper, and blend until smooth.

Serve the dip with vegetable crudités or breadsticks.

Spring Pea Guacamole with Radishes

SERVES 4

1 ripe avocado

7 ounces peas, podded fresh weight or frozen, defrosted if frozen

2 tablespoons chopped mint

½ teaspoon dried red pepper flakes

1 tablespoon crème fraîche

grated zest and juice of 1 lime

sea salt and freshly ground black pepper

12 whole radishes, with leaves on, to serve

The colors and taste of this dish are deliciously fresh and are the very essence of spring. The peas bring a lovely sweetness to the avocado and it's all lightly heated with the pepper flakes. The fresh crunch of the radishes with this pea guacamole is so good and they look so beautiful. You could use other vegetables, like baby carrots, celery, scallions, sugar snaps, or chicory leaves. This is best made on the day as the peas can slightly lose their color in the fridge overnight—but it only takes a few minutes to make, so it's very stress free!

Cut the avocado in half lengthwise and remove the pit, then peel the avocado halves and add to a blender or food processor.

Add all the remaining ingredients except the radishes to the blender or food processor, season with salt and pepper, and blend for about 1 minute until smooth.

Scoop the guacamole into a serving bowl and serve with the radishes.

Spiced Candied Pecans

SERVES 4

2 teaspoons sea salt

½ teaspoon dried thyme

½ teaspoon granulated sugar

¼ teaspoon freshly ground black pepper

¼ teaspoon cayenne pepper

3 tablespoons butter, melted

2 cups raw pecans

These are gorgeous to serve with cocktails. The sweet, salty, and spicy flavors are a delicious coating for the pecans, but you could use almonds or cashews too. I also love making these in big batches to give as gifts—they look so lovely in small mason jars with a handwritten label. They will last for a couple of weeks in an airtight container.

Preheat the oven to 350°F and position a rack in the middle of the oven. Line a baking sheet with parchment paper and set aside.

Place all the ingredients except the butter and pecans in a large bowl and stir to combine. Pour in the melted butter and stir until incorporated, then add the nuts and stir until evenly coated.

Spread the nuts out in a single layer on the lined baking sheet and roast for 15 minutes, stirring once, until golden brown.

Remove from the oven and let cool on the baking sheet, then transfer to a dish and serve.

Smoked Salmon Pâté

SERVES 4

9 ounces smoked salmon, coarsely chopped

½ cup cream cheese

¼ cup crème fraîche

1 teaspoon capers

1 teaspoon finely chopped dill

juice of 1 lemon

sea salt and freshly ground black pepper

very thin slices of bread, toasted, or crackers, to serve

I have been making this smoked salmon pâté for years and this recipe is a particular favorite of mine. I love serving it simply on very thinly sliced sourdough toast or some crispy crackers. It also works perfectly as an appetizer. If you like smoked mackerel, then you can use this exact recipe and just swap out the smoked salmon. I sometimes fold thinly sliced gherkins into the pâté for added flavor and texture. It's so incredibly simple to make—just pop all the ingredients in a food processor and blend!

Place all the ingredients (except the bread) in a blender or food processor, season with salt and pepper, and blend until you have a smooth consistency.

Serve the pâté with very thin toast or crackers.

Smoked Paprika Aioli

MAKES 1 CUP

2 egg yolks

1 tablespoon white wine vinegar

1 teaspoon Dijon mustard

½ cup extra virgin olive oil

½ cup vegetable oil

juice of ½ lemon

½ garlic clove, crushed

1 teaspoon smoked paprika

sea salt and freshly ground black pepper

Put the egg yolks into a bowl, add the vinegar and mustard, and lightly whisk them all together.

Whisk the extra virgin olive and vegetable oils together, then slowly add to the egg yolk mixture, whisking constantly, beginning with a few drops at a time and then in a thin, steady stream when the mixture begins to get thick and creamy.

When all the oil is incorporated, stir in the lemon juice, garlic, and smoked paprika, and season with salt and pepper.

Aged Dubliner Cheese Oat Croquettes with Smoked Paprika Aioli

MAKES 10 CROQUETTES

Cheesy, fluffy croquettes rolled in crunchy oats and then dipped in a lightly spiced aioli is such a delicious snack to serve before a supper party or as a canapé during a party. You can swap out the Dubliner cheese for one of your favorite Cheddars or any good cheese that melts well. I use oats in the crust, but you could use just bread crumbs if you wish and add in some finely ground nuts, like almonds. These can be prepared a day ahead, chilled, and then cooked on the day that you are serving, The croquettes freeze very well too.

3 potatoes, steamed, peeled and mashed (see page 45)

¾ cup aged Dubliner cheese, grated

2 teaspoons Dijon mustard

2 teaspoons finely chopped flat-leaf parsley

sea salt and freshly ground black pepper

½ cup fine fresh bread crumbs

½ cup rolled oats

1 egg, beaten

vegetable oil, for frying

Smoked Paprika Aioli, to serve (see opposite)

Place the mashed potatoes, cheese, mustard, and parsley in a large bowl. Season with salt and pepper and mix together well.

Use a tablespoon to scoop small amounts of the potato mixture, form into balls the size of a ping pong ball, and place on a baking sheet.

Mix the bread crumbs and rolled oats together in a bowl, then spread out on a large plate.

Using a pastry brush, paint the croquettes all over with the beaten egg. Then one by one, gently roll the croquettes in the crumb mixture to coat.

Pour a shallow depth of vegetable oil into a large frying pan and place over medium-high heat.

Once the oil is hot, add the croquettes and fry for a few minutes, turning once, until golden. Alternatively, bake them on a baking sheet in an oven preheated to 400°F for 15 minutes.

Serve the croquettes hot with the smoked paprika aioli.

Pistachio & Rosewater Florentines

MAKES APPROX. 20

These are a staple after-supper treat at most of my suppers. They are without any doubt the most delicious chocolate recipe that I have made and they are so simple to make! It's literally a case of melting, stirring, spooning, sprinkling, and chilling. They take about 15 minutes to make. I sometimes serve them placed on top of a scoop of ice cream, like a fancy hat! There are lots of variations (but this rosewater and pistachio is the best)—orange blossom water with almonds and espresso coffee with hazelnuts or candied orange peel are worth a try. Make them a day ahead and keep chilled. Try to prepare extra if you have time, as people will gobble them up!

10½ ounces dark chocolate (70% cocoa solids), chopped

¾ cup pistachios, finely chopped

1 tablespoon rosewater

¼ ounce dried rose petals

Melt the chocolate in a heatproof bowl set over a saucepan of simmering water (don't let the bottom of the bowl touch the water).

Remove the bowl from the pan and stir half the pistachios and all the rosewater into the melted chocolate.

Place separate tablespoonfuls of the chocolate mixture onto a sheet of parchment paper and form into even-sized rounds.

Sprinkle the remaining pistachios and the dried rose petals on top, then gently press into the melted chocolate. Chill in the fridge for an hour until set.

Chocolate Coconut Truffles

There is nothing quite like a homemade fresh chocolate truffle, and they are so simple to make. I roll the truffles in finely chopped coconut flakes; other variations that I roll them in are finely chopped pistachios, hazelnuts, or almonds. In the chocolate truffle mixture, there are so many delicious flavors I love to add—rosewater, cinnamon, espresso coffee, or cream liqueur. I also make them up for gifts during the holiday season. Make this up a day ahead, and remember to take them out of the fridge at least an hour before serving them so that they are at room temperature.

1¼ cups heavy cream

16 ounces dark chocolate (70% cocoa solids), chopped

¾ cup raw coconut flakes, finely chopped

Pour the cream into a saucepan and bring to a simmer over medium heat.

Place the chocolate in a heatproof bowl. Pour the hot cream all at once over the chocolate, cover, and let sit for about 3 minutes. Then gently stir with a spoon until the mixture is smooth and thoroughly blended.

Let cool to room temperature, stirring occasionally, then chill in the fridge for 3–4 hours until the ganache is thick and quite stiff.

Line a baking sheet with wax or parchment paper and place the coconut flakes in a bowl. Use a tablespoon to scoop small amounts of the ganache and then quickly roll between your palms to form into balls.

Dip the chocolate balls into the coconut flakes until each is coated with the coconut.

Place the truffles on the lined baking sheet and chill in the fridge for at least 1 hour. Remove from the fridge an hour before serving.

Mini Rosemary & Sea Salt Butter Cookies

MAKES 24 COOKIES

I developed this recipe as part of an advertising campaign for Kerrygold butter. I had to come up with the perfect buttery cookie and the best flavor combination. After a few days of experimenting with lots of different quantities of butter and various flavors, in the end this is what we all agreed on being the perfect buttery cookie. The fresh rosemary adds such a delicious sweet, earthy flavor and the sea salt brings that lovely lip-smacking element. I love to make these in little mini versions and serve them with coffee after supper. They are also so cute packaged up as gifts in cellophane bags—tied with a piece of twine and a fresh rosemary sprig.

16 tablespoons (2 sticks) unsalted butter, softened

1 cup superfine sugar

2 teaspoons vanilla extract

1 egg yolk

2 cups all-purpose flour, plus extra for dusting

2 tablespoons finely chopped rosemary leaves

2 teaspoons sea salt

Place the butter, sugar, and vanilla extract in a bowl and beat together until smooth and creamy. Mix in the egg yolk until well-incorporated.

Sift in the flour, add the rosemary and sea salt, and then mix to combine. Scrape onto a lightly floured work surface and knead just until the dough smooths out.

Transfer the dough to a sheet of plastic wrap and roll into a log, then wrap in the plastic wrap and chill in the fridge for an hour.

Preheat the oven to 325°F and line two large baking sheets with parchment paper.

Remove the cookie dough from the fridge, unwrap, and cut into slices about $\frac{1}{8}$-inch thick. Arrange the slices on the lined baking sheets about 1 inch apart (they won't be spreading very much, but they need room for air to circulate around them).

Bake for about 12 minutes until only just beginning to turn golden around the edges.

Remove from the oven and let cool on the baking sheet before eating. Store in an airtight container for up to one week.

Cheeseboard

HOW TO CREATE A CHEESEBOARD

When I am putting together a large cheeseboard, I gather together cheeses that have different textures and flavors. There are five different categories of cheese—soft, fresh, blue, hard, and semisoft, and I usually stick with getting one of each. I like to lay out all my cheeses on a big wooden cutting board before my guests arrive, and place it on a sideboard with a light cotton cloth or kitchen towel loosely laid on top—just to protect the cheeses.

I always serve a chutney with my cheeseboard, and I have a house Spicy Apple Chutney that I have made for years. I think it's lovely to serve a homemade chutney—try your hand at making mine (see opposite). But of course there are lots of interesting chutneys that you can buy, such as onion jam, fig chutney, pear chutney, and so on. I also serve apple slices, as they are a great palate cleanser in between cheeses. A big bunch of red grapes also work to freshen the palate, and their sweetness really complements the cheese. When figs are in season, I lay them on my cheeseboard as they go so well with many varieties of cheese.

I serve oatcakes with my cheeses, as they have a wonderful crumbly texture and cereal flavor that is the perfect undertone to all different cheeses. Do try my recipe for Rosemary Oatcakes (see opposite), but substitute any cracker.

When I am having a small supper, I just serve one special cheese. When it's just one cheese, you can really spend the time selecting something interesting and finding out about where and how it was made, so that you can share it with your friends over supper.

Remember to you take the cheese out of the fridge at least a couple of hours before serving, to bring the cheese to room temperature, so it will taste its best. And pour a lovely glass of port for all your friends to create the perfect cheese course.

Rosemary Oatcakes

MAKES 20

¼ teaspoon baking powder

¾ cup warm water

5 tablespoons butter, melted

2¾ cups rolled oats

⅔ cup whole wheat flour, plus extra for dusting

1 tablespoon finely chopped rosemary

1 teaspoon sea salt

2 tablespoons superfine sugar

Preheat the oven to 350°F.

Dissolve the baking powder in the warm water and whisk in the melted butter.

Place the oats, flour, rosemary, salt, and sugar in a large bowl and mix together.

Pour the liquid into the dry ingredients, stirring as you pour to make a stiff dough.

Lightly dust a clean work surface with a little flour and roll out the dough to about ¼-inch thick. Cut out 20 x 2-inch circles using a pastry cutter.

Arrange on lined baking sheets and bake for 35 minutes until pale golden. Turn the oatcakes over in the oven after 25 minutes. Cool on a wire rack. Store in an airtight container for up to two weeks.

Spicy Apple Chutney

MAKES 12 X 8-OUNCE JARS

6½ pounds cooking apples, peeled, quartered, and cored

3 onions

5 tablespoons butter

2¾ cups dark brown sugar

20 cloves

2 tablespoons chile powder

2 tablespoons ground turmeric

5-inch piece of fresh ginger, peeled and grated

2½ cups cider vinegar

sea salt and freshly ground black pepper

I started making this chutney to sell at the farmers' markets in Ireland over 16 years ago. It is the best chutney I have ever made and there is always a jar in my kitchen! The perfect time to make it is when apples are in season, so that is when I make big batches—usually 30 or 40 jars. It lasts for about six months stored in a cool, dark place, so you can enjoy it throughout the whole year. The flavors are sweet and spicy—so work perfectly with cheeses, pâtés, and cold meats.

Chop the apples into small chunks and dice the onions.

Place a large saucepan over low heat and melt the butter. Stir in the apples and onions followed by the brown sugar, cloves, chile powder, turmeric, ginger, and vinegar, and season with salt and pepper. Mix well. Cover the saucepan, increase the heat, and bring to a boil. Reduce the heat and let simmer over medium heat for 20 minutes, stirring every 5 minutes.

Remove the lid, reduce the heat, and let cook for another 30 minutes until the apples have broken down and the chutney has turned a rich, golden brown. Use the back of a wooden spoon to crush the apples. Remove the pan from the heat and let cool; the chutney will thicken more as it cools.

Once the chutney has cooled, spoon it into 12 sterilized jars, seal, and label.

Rosemary Clodagh Bread

MAKES 1 LOAF

No matter which supper I am cooking, I always serve this bread in the center of the table and I ask my guests to break the bread with me. This is a big tradition in my home; for me, it symbolizes the beginning of the supper, a shared and peaceful offering. It is a very simple bread to make, because there is no kneading or resting involved. It's a take on the traditional Irish soda bread—it's wholesome and crumbly but doesn't leave you feeling bloated like yeast breads can. It takes 20 minutes to prepare and then it's straight in the oven.

1½ cups bread flour, plus extra for dusting

2 teaspoons baking soda

3 cups whole wheat flour

2 tablespoons finely chopped rosemary

1 teaspoon sea salt

1½ cups milk

1 cup plain yogurt

milk and yogurt mix, for brushing

Preheat your oven to 425°F.

Sift the white flour and baking soda into a large mixing bowl and stir in the whole wheat flour, one tablespoon of finely chopped fresh rosemary, and the sea salt. Using clean hands, mix the dry ingredients together and make a well in the center of the bowl.

Whisk together the yogurt and milk and slowly pour into the well of the dry ingredients. Use your free hand to mix the dough lightly, spreading your fingers far apart. Make sure that there are no dry patches and that the dough is completely wet.

Pat your hands with flour and shape the dough into one round. Place on a floured baking sheet. Flour a large knife and cut the shape of a cross into the top of the dough about two-thirds of the way through.

Brush the round of bread with the milk and yogurt mixture using a pastry brush—this will give a lovely golden color to the bread once baked—and sprinkle the remaining chopped rosemary on top.

Bake for 25 minutes, then reduce the heat to 350°F for another 25 minutes. To test whether the loaf is cooked, tap the bottom with your knuckles; it should sound hollow. Let cool on a cooling rack.

Index

Acknowledgments

I want to start by thanking Kyle Cathie, one of the most dedicated publishers in this business who is now retired. She made sure to get this book commissioned before she left, always believing in me and the ideas that I have. Thank you Kyle from the bottom of my heart. You are missed...

Dora Kazmierak, the photographer for this book. Dora has been a friend of mine for many years and has put endless hours into helping me create this very special book. Dora, you are so talented and I love watching you grow and grow. Excited that this is your first book, hooray!

Lizzie Harris, who cooked all the delicious dishes in the book. Lizzie, I absolutely adore you! You are the most talented chef and kindest person. Thank you for putting so much care into making each recipe look so good!

Vicky Orchard, the editor. Thank you Vicky for keeping me on track and arranging so much to make this a joy to work on.

Lucy Gowans, the designer. Thank you for making the pages look so beautiful and perfectly aligned! Wei Tang, the props stylist. Thank you for gathering so many beautiful props for me to play with!

Harry Herbert, my amazing boyfriend. Thank you for the hours you have spent reading over this book and finding all my little mistakes, for eating all my recipes, and for being a constant positive voice. I love you with all my heart.

To all my dear friends. Hannah Pawlby, Anoushka Healy, Thea Rogers, Fiona Leahy, Nikki Tibbles, Sally Greene, my sister Mairead McKenna, plus many more. Thank you all so much for your support from the very beginning when I first started to try to get this book published. For giving me so much advice, and for eating all my dishes with enthusiasm! You are all such a massive part of this book. I am very lucky to have you all...

And to you, for buying this book, cooking the recipes, and sharing my love for suppers at home.

Love, Clo xxx